MW01165409

MONEY, MURDER, AND MADNESS

A BANKING LIFE

How Your Government Caused The Financial Crisis

FORREST RUSSELL COOK

authorHOUSE®

AuthorHouse™
1663 Liberty Drive
Bloomington, IN 47403
www.authorhouse.com
Phone: 1-800-839-8640

Published by AuthorHouse 02/03/2015

ISBN: 978-1-4969-5961-4 (sc)
ISBN: 978-1-4969-5962-1 (hc)
ISBN: 978-1-4969-5960-7 (e)

Library of Congress Control Number: 2015900054

To June,
It's been a wonderful journey because of you

Contents

Part III: An Exploration and Analysis Of The Recent Financial Crisis

Introduction

I was introduced recently by a friend as an "unindicted banker." In my early days I made a number of visits to Bank of America in San Francisco for credit card meetings before Bank of America moved to Charlotte, North Carolina. The headquarters was in a new impressive tower building with a large plaza in front. There was a black sculpture of no particular shape prominently displayed on the plaza.

I noticed a group of people taking pictures one day and I heard one of them say, "I think they call it the banker's heart." A lot of people say they hate bankers and I tried not to take it personally.

During my years in banking I received death threats and hate mail and I encountered pickets and demonstrations.

Banking was not the way many politicians and members of the media described it. I worked with people I was proud to be associated with and many of them were outstanding women.

There were very few women officers or department heads in the early days at the Rockland-Atlas Bank and at State Street Bank. I unhappily recall that all the men smoked at their desks and in their offices. Although I never saw any written prohibition or heard any verbal instructions--it was accepted that women did not smoke while working. The unequal treatment rapidly gave way to a more level playing field when it became apparent there was a need for more talented and competent people. When I retired from South Shore Bank we had thirty-five to forty senior women officers and department heads. Our branch offices were mostly managed by women who were given considerable personal authority.

State Street Bank was a wonderful organization when I was there and it grew into a world-class financial company; however, being in a community bank like Bank of New Hampshire or South Shore Bank was special. Employees and customers were on a first name basis and we loved being involved in the life of the community. Unfortunately community banks are becoming a thing of the past due to mergers. Relationships are less personal and decision-making often remote.

All businesses change over time. The banking business changed during the time I was working, but in recent years the pace of change has dramatically increased and the electronic world in many ways is making traditional banking obsolete. I started as a trainee at the Rockland-Atlas Bank in Boston and I retired almost forty years later after an adventure I could not have imagined on the first day I signed on as a "banker."

The first part of this book is about my personal journey in banking. It includes many great people, a few villains and the murder of a Boston police officer at one of our branches. I also wrote that I was fired as chief executive officer of Bank of New Hampshire by the family who owned the bank, in spite of the fact the bank was an outstanding performer.

The second part is how our banking system evolved, no other country does it quite like we do. The Bank of England was established in 1694. Our two early attempts to have a central-bank ended in failure. The Federal Reserve was created in 1913 and it's 100th anniversary was in December 2013. The debate continues whether the Fed has been a success or failure. It's curious that the Fed did not originate in the halls of Congress or in the White House. The Fed was conceived at J.P. Morgan's private club at Jekyll Island, Georgia.

The third part is controversial. I believe our government caused the housing collapse that led to the financial crisis. The elected and appointed officials most responsible have been skillful at blaming others. It may be old news to some but if we do not know the facts it's highly likely the same mistakes will be repeated.

Part I

From Boston To Fort Kent

Chapter 1

A Personal Journey In Banking

In 1958, after two years in the pharmaceutical business, I was looking for a career in banking. My timing was not good. We were in the middle of a recession and several interviews were not productive.

I happened to be standing on Congress Street in Boston with not much on my schedule when I noticed the Rockland-Atlas Bank across the street. It didn't appear as imposing as The First National Bank or the Shawmut Bank and the name seemed a little strange for a Boston bank. I hadn't done any research or checked with my two uncles in the banking business, but the thought was very much on my mind; my wife was pregnant with our first child and it would be nice to go home and say, "Honey, I have a job!"

I walked in the front door of the Rockland-Atlas Bank and said to someone I was looking for a job. Instead of sending me to Personnel, as it was known in those days and later Human Resources, I was introduced to Heinie Dellicker, Vice President of the Commercial Division. I was quite sure interviewing guys off the street was not in his job description. Fortunately we hit it off immediately. He introduced me to Roy Lawson, the banks only senior vice president, and to Hop Haydock, Vice President of Commercial Lending and to several others. Haydock was brilliant and kind of unpredictable. I enjoyed working for him later on. I had the feeling things were going quite well but you never know. I was increasingly impressed with how enthusiastic everyone was about the bank.

Before I left several hours later Heinie said, "don't call me Mister," and he took me aside and said it was unanimous that they wanted to hire me and I should report to Bob Northup in Personnel to set up a training program. "What no training program?"

My visit with Bob Northup was as enjoyable as my first day with Heinie Delicker. Bob Northup and I became very good friends and I regularly asked for his advice and guidance, even after I left the bank.

Northup said, "I know there are only a few days left in the year, but if you start tomorrow we can give you your regular two weeks vacation, but also give you full pay when you are on active duty for two weeks with the army reserve in the summer. My salary was set at $5,500 for the year so his thoughtfulness was greatly appreciated.

I was assigned to the Credit Department for my personalized training program. It was demanding and thorough. We analyzed company financial reports and reviewed our work with Chet Patterson who was the head of the department. Patterson required absolute honesty even if risked offending the loan officer. The final step was a meeting with the loan officer responsible for the account. The meetings were often intense.

Chapter 2

Early Years At Rockland-Atlas Bank

In something less than a year I began calling on customers in Maine with Dick Brackett, Assistant Vice President. We both had graduated from Bowdoin College and loved the state of Maine. We had a very agreeable association and he readily shared his several years of experience.

On one trip to Maine we thought it was funny when we crossed the border between New Hampshire and Maine, it was sunny and spring like but beyond Augusta it was late fall, and later in the day in Presque Isle it was like mid-winter.

From Fort Kent on the Canadian border to Kittery there is a vast territory and I found it exciting that an assistant vice president and his side-kick, a non officer who still had to punch a time clock (which incidentally turned from blue ink to screaming red if you were late), were responsible for such a large book of business.

On another occasion I was away from the bank at a convention of Maine Bankers. I left home early on Thursday morning and returned Sunday afternoon. I sent in my time card with a notation, regular hours. A person in personnel sent it back with strict instructions to record actual hours

I consulted with my boss, Hop Haydock, and he laughed and said, "Well give them what they want, it's going to be a good paycheck." I immediately became the only non-officer exception to punching the clock.

We were traveling to Maine on one of our regular visits and Dick told me in absolute confidence that I would be promoted to assistant treasurer at the board meeting that week. He emphasized he shouldn't be jumping the gun, but he couldn't wait to share the good news with me.

As we called on customers and prospects in northern Maine, especially bankers, we kept hearing that Rockland-Atlas and State Street were engaged in merger talks. We thought it would be a good idea to check with headquarters. We were told there was no truth to the rumors and to get back to calling on customers. When we got back to Boston it was no longer a rumor. A merger was under way.

By the way, at the board meeting that week my promotion was forgotten. I learned early in the game mergers can be difficult.

Well, the merger took place. Rockland-Atlas was the smaller organization, and some of our new friends tried to make sure we understood who was in charge. Fred Hagemann, President and CEO of Rockland-Atlas, became the new president and CEO of State Street Bank. Guess who was really in charge?

It was a very different world in the early 60s. England, Europe, Italy and Japan were not fully recovered from the ravages of World War II. The United States stood alone.

I remember Barney Frank who has been around for a long time, saying in several speeches, the only competition we had were Swiss watches and chocolate.

Many of the senior guys I worked with were World War II veterans. They seemed committed to making every minute count. They worked hard and did not hold back when it was time to have fun.

We did a lot of entertaining at lunches, dinners and conventions. It's true martini lunches were common. You see some unusual behavior at conventions. My wife June and I were fortunate that State Street policy encouraged husbands and wives to be together as much as possible when entertaining customers.

We had some good times with Jack and Noreen Ahern at conventions. Jack was head of the Investment Division and I worked closely with him and many of our correspondent bank customers. I've forgotten where the convention was being held when I asked if they were going. He said no, the trip was too long. I learned later he had flown many missions as a B17 bomber pilot over Germany during the war. After returning home he vowed never to set foot in a plane again. If he couldn't get there by car he didn't go.

Hop Haydock stole a train, a whole damn train, and went for a joy ride in wartime France. Someone must have seen the same thing I saw, he was just too valuable to put in a stockade.

Lew Farley was head of the International Department, that part of the business was relatively small but growing. Lew was soft spoken, rather scholarly and not one you heard a lot from at meetings, but he had the information and skills that very few had. You probably would not have guessed he was a submarine commander and had survived many war time patrols in the Pacific.

My closest friend during my State Street years and all the years thereafter was Stan Lang. He served in the army in France and Germany during the war.

Ned Roberts was another hard-working guy and a real character. We were on the second floor on Congress Street, it wasn't a very large space, maybe fifteen of us in Commercial Lending. Ned arrived early as usual one morning but this time he had his dog with him. The dog had a wonderful time visiting all of us and Ned then tied his dog's leash to his desk. Ned left for lunch and didn't come back. After awhile Ned's secretary said that she would take the dog for a walk on the Common. The next day the dog dutifully took his spot under the desk. When Ned didn't show up several of us asked Anne if she knew what was going on and she said she didn't. Late in the day Ned returned, greeted his dog, and they went home together. The funny thing was none of us thought this was unusual. I look back at those days with appreciation for the friendship and wonderful experiences I shared with such an incredible group of guys.

Chapter 3

State Street Bank

After the merger with State Street I was assigned to the Correspondent Banking Department. Don Lewis was head of the department and it was generally believed he would be the next head of the Retail Division. There was one other vice president from the Rockland-Atlas Bank who was a few years away from retirement.

Joe Robbins, the vice president from the Rockland-Bank and I became good friends and we made many business calls together. Joe had a lot of excellent contacts. Our customer calls were generally built around long very interesting lunches. There were two other assistant vice presidents from State Street, one whose father was a director of the bank.

It didn't look promising, I was the only non-officer. My friend Brackett didn't fare much better. He soon left to join another bank.

Lewis was personally responsible for a large number of very good accounts in Maine. We spent a week together calling on his customers and when we got back to Boston he said, "Well it's all yours now, good luck." I had so much business they had to promote me.

My wife and I traveled all over the country, including Hawaii, with Don and Mary Lewis for banking conventions, meetings and dinners. It was a wonderful adventure and we remained devoted friends until both Don and Mary passed away.

Don Lewis had many years of experience in the banking business and he was very careful not to do anything that would embarrass the bank but an unusual event happened at the Wentworth Hotel in New Castle,

New Hampshire. The Smiths owned the hotel at the time and had become embroiled in a personal battle with the local police chief. The chief went out of his way to harass the hotel guests.

The chief deliberately escalated a minor incident into a confrontation. He demanded that Lewis remove his car from a public parking space across from the hotel and when Lewis asked why he was promptly arrested and taken to jail.

My assignment was to get him released quickly and have the record erased. I knew a prominent local attorney in Portsmouth who represented one of our correspondent bank customers and I asked him if he could help.

I paid him a large fee, which my boss promptly reimbursed. Lewis was released without any record of the incident. It was an up close and personal event that I witnessed about how a government official used his authority to unreasonably and unlawfully punish people he didn't like. Unfortunately I would see government officials doing similar things in the years ahead.

I worked hard and loved what I was doing. Several promotions came along quite quickly. Fred Hagemann was an outstanding leader who set the highest example for moral and ethical behavior. It was a great way to start in business.

A group of us met with the boss one day for an informal discussion. I think some would be surprised to hear he didn't spend a lot of time on the company mission or his vision. One of the things I remember has stayed with me all these years. He said, " You know we expect you to work hard and you should commit to life-long learning, but don't forget you are a privileged group. I want you to find time in your busy lives to give something back to the communities where we do business and where you live. If you are willing to plant shade trees under which you may never sit you will know what I mean." I brought his message with me wherever I went.

In the early years at State Street I attended the Massachusetts Banking School at Williams College, the Stonier School of Banking at Rutgers University and the Advanced Management Program at Harvard Business School. At Harvard we lived in so-called "Can" groups. We worked long hours, including many Saturdays and peer pressure was quite intense.

I was very fortunate to room with Wookie Kotzie. Wookie was from Zimbabwe and he managed a copper mine with over 2000 employees. He was a quiet kind of person with a great intellect. When we had a few days off he came home with me and became part of our family. One weekend it was his birthday so we sang "Happy Birthday" to him which brought tears to his eyes. He went around the table and hugged each of us! He was a truly good person and I miss him very much.

Chapter 4

Correspondent Banking

Correspondent banking is not a well known form of the business and it has changed substantially over the years. In the sixties and seventies banks were much smaller than they are today. There were fewer holding companies and greater restrictions on mergers and branch banking.

When I began traveling throughout the state of Maine I was surprised how modest in size the Portland Maine banks were. The small to medium-size commercial banks, savings banks, and savings and loans maintained demand deposits (checking accounts that did not pay interest) with various correspondent banks that were members of the Fed.

The demand deposits, often of considerable size, where extremely valuable to the correspondent bank and were aggressively solicited. In return for the deposits the correspondent bank received various services such as check collection, safekeeping of securities, trading in government bonds, investment advice and delivery of cash and coin. All of the services, except investment advice is a regular Federal Reserve service.

There was another important service provided by correspondent banks like State Street. We participated in over-loans, that is loans that exceeded the lending limit of a local bank.

The local bank could make a loan over its limit to a local customer, retain the relationship and participate the excess amount to a bank like State Street. Sometimes when the over limit was particularly large we wrote the loan directly and participated back the local bank's share. It was a relationship that was beneficial to both parties.

One time I brought back a tax participation note from a small Maine town that looked like it was on the back of an envelope. It took some convincing with our investment people that it was a good loan because I knew the selectmen who signed it.

We did a large volume of interbank loans every year and never had a loss. Inevitably banks became larger over the years and more loans were retained by the local banks.

The Monetary Control Act of 1980 required all depository institutions, member banks and nonmember banks, savings and loans, savings banks and even credit unions to maintain reserves at the Fed. The Fed, supposedly above politics, had secured the prize in consolidating it's institutional power. Correspondent banking started disappearing.

The Banking Act of 1933, generally known as the Glass-Steagall Act is well-known for separating commercial banking and investment banking. There is an important provision of the Act that is less well remembered today, banks were prohibited from paying interest on checking account deposits.

Two widely held theories were given for the prohibition of interest on demand deposits. First, it was believed that banks sought high-risk loans to cover the cost of the interest payments. Second, banks in Federal Reserve cities employed large correspondent balances in overnight loans. In times of difficulty it was thought that the withdrawal of interbank deposits caused undue stress on the market.

Studies at the time and later found no merit in either theory. No one listened. The Federal Deposit Insurance Corporation was a creation of the Glass-Steagall Act.

The Act provided government insurance for the banks checking and savings accounts. The cost of the insurance was one half percent on these deposits. Rates were very low at the time, so the interest cost to the banks was large.

It's likely the large city banks agreed to the insurance provision of the Act in exchange for the inclusion of a prohibition on interest rate payments on checking accounts. It would be seventy-five years before the law was changed.

Chapter 5

A Bare Bones Christmas

The Skowhegan Savings Bank in Maine was a typical correspondent bank customer at State Street Bank, except for the fact the Chairman of the Board, Blin Page regularly maintained a personal checking account with us of more than one million dollars. The bank also carried demand deposit balances of one or two million dollars. It was a time when only commercial banks could offer demand deposits (checking accounts) and large accounts were extremely valuable. Fred Hagemann who was president of State Street Bank, regularly asked me if I was taking good care of Mr. Page and the people at the savings bank.

Mr. Page was not active in the day to day management of the bank, but I saw him regularly in Skowhegan, Maine. He and Mrs. Page often visited us in Boston. We had a branch bank in the Statler Hotel in Boston and the Pages often stayed at the hotel. He enjoyed cashing a check for a modest amount and watching the tellers reaction when she checked his account balance.

I usually arrived at the Skowhegan Bank no later than 7:05 a.m. Fortunately I enjoyed a good relationship with everyone at the bank. Management was ultraconservative in investing and lending and at one time they ran into an earnings squeeze.

Mr. Page called and asked me to arrange a meeting with Fred Hagemann. Hagemann was a highly regarded banker an expert bond man from his earlier days at Boatman's Bank in St. Louis.

Mr. Page and I had a good meeting with Hagemann and he suggested that Page and I visit with Preston Breed, Senior Vice President in charge of real estate lending. I was an assistant vice president at the time and most of us who were "junior officers" found Breed condescending and difficult to deal with. I had reservations about working with him, but I thought with Hagemann's involvement it would be okay.

It's a long story, but basically one of Breed"s customers, the A. B. Smith Trust Company, (not its real name) in Phoenix, Arizona agreed to send me a large package of government insured real estate loans, registered in the Skowhegan Bank's name.

I was horrified at the poor quality of almost every loan in the package. I went to see Breed to express my concern. In his usual manner he said, "You don't understand, Phoenix is a frontier and the loans will look different from what you would expect. He added there shouldn't be a problem because the loans are insured." I said that may be but our friends in Skowhegan have never had a default and these loans will go bad in massive numbers.

The next day one of Breeds associates told me they had just had a conference call with Smith in Arizona and they thought it was very funny that Smith had sent me a package of culls (rejected loans). It was late on a Friday afternoon and Breed was nowhere to be found.

I called Smith in Arizona and was told he was at his hunting lodge for the weekend and could not be disturbed. I protested but couldn't get through. I took the package to the post office and included an explicit note of what I thought of Smith and his company. When I got home I told my wife it was likely I would be looking for a new job on Monday.

Monday morning all hell broke lose. Breed wanted me fired! I met with several senior officers but noted there was great reluctance to draw Hagemann into the discussion. I don't know what was said when I wasn't in the room and I never mentioned it to Fred Hagemann. I survived and we found other ways to help our friends in Maine. I was disappointed to learn State Street paid a lot of money to A. B. Smith for the trouble.

I kept my file for a period of time and subsequently learned Smith was found guilty on fraud charges and served time in jail. No one ever mentioned it to me.

I hasten to add it was an isolated incident; the people I worked with from Woody Woodworth who was in charge of all lending, and all the others at State Street, without exception, were very ethical and completely honest.

After several years I received word from my friends in Skowhegan that

Mr. Page had died. It was a bitter cold day when I drove up for the funeral. The day before the funeral I visited Mrs. Page at an unpretentious Victorian home near the center of town. I was surprised she was alone. We had tea and talked for awhile. She was really a grand lady. Before I left I asked if I could do anything for her and to please call me in the future if I could be helpful. She hesitated and then said, "Mr. Page," (she always referred to him as mister), "told me to call you and our attorney in Waterville if anything happened to him." She said she was a little concerned if she had enough money in her household account. I told her I had checked before leaving Boston and the balance in their joint checking was about $822,000 and I could transfer whatever amount she wanted to her local account. I also said it would be a good idea to call her attorney in Waterville when it was convenient. I assume she knew they owned vast tracts of timberland as well as other very valuable assets. She seemed to be very relieved to know she had sufficient funds for her household account.

The next day was a grey and cold and there was no gathering following the funeral service. I said goodbye to Mrs. Page again.

As I was leaving town I noticed a farm house on the ridge line with flames shooting out of the chimney. I drove up to the house and knocked on the door and a woman answered. She had no idea that flames were pouring out of the chimney and cinders were landing on the roof. The house was badly in need of care and looked like a tinder box. I asked her to call the fire department and she ran away, then came back and said she didn't have a phone. At that point I was in the kitchen where there was a wooden table, two wooden chairs and a live chicken!

I could see a day bed with a young child in the next room and a Christmas tree. This was going to be a bare bones Christmas. I said to her to please get the kids dressed and I would go next door to call for help. It took the fire department only a few minutes to arrive but somewhat longer to extinguish the fire.

I took a young girl and young boy out into the barn to escape the soot and activity in the house. The young boy only had sneakers on his feet. He proudly pulled back a tarp to show me his father's boat which appeared to be new and expensive. He told me his father was a good fisherman and was logging in the woods and would not be back until the weekend.

The firemen left and one of them told me it was a close call. I was still there and now there was no heat in the house. The mother said she had to go to work in the diner or she wouldn't have any money for Christmas. I told her she couldn't leave the kids there or they would freeze to death. We piled into my car looking for a place for the kids to stay for a couple of hours and I was relieved to hear her mother would be home from the shoe factory so they could spend the night with her. We located a girlfriend who seemed very nice and the kids looked happy. I dropped the mother off at the diner, which was within walking distance from her house, and she said that any time I was in Skowhegan she would like to buy me a cup of coffee.

We looked at each other and wished each other a Merry Christmas!

Maine is a beautiful state, most people know it's magnificent coastline or vacation spots, but if you drive a few miles inland or way up north it's a very different place. Some of the best and most generous people I ever met were off the beaten path in places like, Skowhegan, Squaw Pan Dam, Mars Hill, Ashland, South Paris and Sanford. Not all the lessons I learned were about balance sheets and profit and loss statements.

Chapter 6

State Street Bank, A Pioneer In Credit Cards

My boss Don Lewis moved up to head the Retail Division which at the time was called Depositors Service Division and I succeeded him as head of Correspondent Banking. Hagemann retired and the board went outside for a new Chief Executive Officer. George Rockwell joined us from IBM.

Hagemann and Rockwell were very different personalities and they each had their own management styles, but both were very effective leaders. It was not long before our culture became less old Boston banking and more entrepreneurial and competitive.

Don Lewis was a big imposing guy but he hated speaking in front of groups. Fortunately for me he designated me the spokesman for the division at our annual long-range planning meetings.

The meetings were two day sessions at some great locations away from Boston. They were intense and competitive and a lot of fun. We felt the need for some showmanship, but it was critical to gain general approval from your peers as well as the boss. We understood each of us was competing for the allocation of capital and other resources to expand our part of the business.

Massachusetts banks at the time were restricted to having offices only in the county where the main office was located. State Street had eighteen offices in Boston and Suffolk County. Although Boston was the capitol and Suffolk County is densely populated it's a small geographical area. I often said I could see all of our offices from the top floor of our building.

Bank of America had over one thousand offices in California, Washington and Oregon. It was a retail giant in banking. At the planning meetings Lewis and I urged the adoption of Shawmut's model for our long-range plan.

Shawmut over a period of years had acquired a number of very good banks throughout the Commonwealth via their holding company. I had good relationships with most CEOs of the independent banks and I was sure we could convince many of them to join as a member of the State Street Holding Company.

Although the plan was never formally rejected it required significant capital commitments and a relatively long range time frame. Several meetings that I arranged with George Rockwell and CEOs of banks that were potential merger possibilities did not go well and did not promise great success.

Several of us formed a small committee to develop new products and services but we really needed a breakthrough. The opportunity came from an unexpected source.

Bank of America representatives visited us with a proposal to join them as a franchise bank in a new credit card program called BankAmericard. State Street being a franchise bank we would own the relationships and pay BofA a fee.

We assumed they had tried First National Bank of Boston and Shawmut before visiting us as both had much larger retail outlets and were probably turned down.

BofA had experimented with a credit card program in the early 1950's in the Bay Area, but quickly abandoned it because of credit and fraud losses. The plan also lacked broad appeal because it covered such a restricted area.

The appeal to us was the great size of BofA and what appeared to be a full commitment to make it a national plan. Chase Bank joined as one of the first major banks.

As unlikely as State Street was to make such a high risk leap into unknown territory, we signed on as one of the earliest franchise banks.

Credit cards in the early days did not have an electronic stripe on the back of the card. You may remember purchasing something and seeing salespersons looking through reams of computer paper, including the "hot card report." It was clumsy and not user friendly. The scam artists had a field day as credit and fraud losses sky rocketed.

Our BankAmericard Department was losing money at an alarming rate. George Rockwell, President, had supported our entry into the business and said to me, "you were a major supporter of the card business so you're now in charge of the BankAmericard task force – pick whomever you want, fix the problems and make it profitable or close it down!"

I was only a few months away from succeeding my boss, Don Lewis, as Retail Division head and this didn't look good! It didn't take long to uncover fraudulent reporting to coverup a situation that was substantially worse than anyone knew, including our directors.

It was a bad situation which required the removal of several officers and supervisors. I asked the head of internal audit for the Bank to join me in my initial report to Rockwell. The meeting was brief and I was made the new head of the credit card department.

I left the main office for an old building on Tremont Street. Most of my colleagues thought they would never see me again.

I knew I was in trouble when I went in early Saturday morning and found my new team playing stickball in the middle of the office. I called the game because of inclement weather!

As I was going back to my office I looked out on a flat roof and saw an unpleasant looking fellow dropping bricks down a vent. I shouted at him to stop and he gave me a rude hand signal and kept on dropping bricks. It was a leased building so I called the superintendent and decided to go home for the weekend since it would all be there Monday morning. Maybe.

My visits to the board meetings were difficult because I didn't have enough good answers to their questions. Several directors were insistent that we cut our losses and close the business. I was happy they said their criticism was not directed at me, but I thought if the business goes down failure would be attached to me and I would go down with it.

When I moved to Tremont Street I knew something about consumer credit but virtually nothing about credit cards; the problem was no one else did either. The only ones who knew anything about bank cards were at Bank of America.

I spent a week with the people at BofA and at their recommendation I visited Dee Hock at the National Bank of Commerce in Oregon. Hock would soon become a rising star in the credit card business. A short while later I joined a BankAmericard marketing committee and made many visits to BofA.

It was encouraging to escape the negative atmosphere at the home office and participate in meetings that were energetic and enthusiastic.

The technology group reported on several very important innovations that would be available in the near future. It proved to be not just hopeful talk.

My hope was to convince Rockwell and the directors not to give up too soon. I kept repeating "if we're just given a little more time there would be breakthroughs and we'll make the business profitable."

Back home things were not all bad. I found we had many good people who did things professionally and took pride in their work. I brought in an experienced retail credit manager from the Retail Division. I also was very fortunate to find Guy Santagate who was the Sales and Marketing Manager. He was a person of high intelligence and energy and had a wonderful sense of humor, something we badly needed.

The early days in the business were grim and I know I would not have made it without Guy. The credit card business would not have survived without him. Santagate was the person who developed our agent bank system. A number of New England banks joined us as agents. They made the card available to their customers and received fees but the cardholders belonged to State Street.

Although it was not part of our plan I reminded my boss George Rockwell and our directors that any discussion to close down the business should include our responsibility not to harm our agent banks that had joined us in good faith

In addition to thousands of cardholders who had never done business with us, we also signed thousands of merchants that accepted State Street BankAmericard. By entering the credit card business we were able to extend banking services to individuals and businesses well beyond the legal restriction of only having branch offices in Suffolk County.

BankAmericard in the beginning was a part of the Consumer Group of Bank of America. The franchise banks were unhappy and some mutinous about the decision making process including my boss Rockwell, who was on the committee of franchise banks.

BofA finally made the decision to sell the business and the BankAmerica trademark to National Bank of America with Dee Hock as chief executive.

Hock was a true visionary; he and his group revolutionized the back office payments system. There are several parties to a card transaction; the card-issuing bank, the card holders, the entity accepting the card, the clearing organization and the owner of the trademark. It's a complex system that went from a cumbersome paper system to a speed-of-light electronics system. Dee Hock made it work!

The major breakthrough came with the development of the electronic stripe on the back of the card. It works from almost anywhere in the world and provides valuable current information on the status of the cardholder. It's not perfect but enough to greatly reduce credit and fraud losses.

Hock quickly did two things to rebrand the business. He moved out of the BofA building to an equally grand tower across the street and he renamed the business VISA.

Hock had hoped to eliminate much of the complaining from the early days by having a board made up exclusively of CEOs from franchise banks; Rockwell was one. It was a good idea but it produced a board of directors as strong-willed as himself.

There was criticism of the elaborate office and library he built for himself and his increasingly dictatorial style. He was reported to have said when calling for a vote, "all in favor say aye, those opposed leave the room." The unrest was enough that he retired to his ranch and disappeared from the business he was instrumental in creating.

Don Lewis retired and I returned to the main office as head of the Retail Division. Guy Santagate took over the VISA Card operation.

Along with becoming a division head I served on the senior management committee, the long range planning committee and acquisition committee, so I had ample opportunity to promote retail banking; however State Street was steadily moving in a different direction.

Chapter 7

On To New Hampshire

After sixteen good years at State Street Bank I was growing a little restless. I knew the reason was State Street was moving away from a retail banking model and more toward investment and mutual fund business. It was a good bank when I was there and it became a world class bank in later years.

Bank of America, the country's largest bank, was still focused on retail banking. Chase, CitiBank and J. P. Morgan and other banking giants were also expanding retail banking.

During my correspondent banking years I became good friends with many New England bank presidents. I had several interesting opportunities to leave State Street; one was to start a companion bank for a large mutual fund, but for one reason or another I didn't pursue any of them.

Dave Thurber, Chairman of Bank of New Hampshire, called and asked me to have lunch with him in Boston. BNH was a recent combination of three banks, one in Concord, another in Manchester, and Thurber's bank in Nashua. I had known Davis Thurber for years and I had a very high regard for him. The new bank sounded like a great idea and had the potential to be a real force in New Hampshire.

Mergers are never easy and the three-way merger was proving to be very difficult. Thurber told me the three cultures were at war with each other and the price of the stock in the new bank was taking a beating and they were barely covering the dividend. The directors were mutinous and had reached the decision to go outside for a new president.

Although the idea of being president of BNH had a lot of appeal, one would have to be naïve not to realize there was a potential management problem if the duties of the chairman and president were not clearly defined and agreed to by both parties.

The Thurber family owned a very large block of stock in the bank. Davis Thurber's grandfather had started the bank. Dave Thurber, his brother and cousin were Directors and permanent members of the Executive Committee. After several meetings with various directors and family members, Thurber and I reached an agreement. Thurber made the motion at the next board meeting to elect me President and Chief Executive Officer and the vote was unanimous.

Dave Thurber and I worked very well together for five years. I respected his substantial ownership position and his role as chairman. He in turn gave me complete support as CEO. I also enjoyed a very good relationship with his cousin who was a major shareholder, director and member of the executive committee.

During my time at Bank of New Hampshire I had the opportunity to meet Senator Tom McIntyre a number of times. He was fifteenth or sixteenth in seniority and had considerable influence on banking legislation.

I hadn't been at BNH very long when a thunderbolt hit. Ron Haseltine, President of Consumers Savings Bank in Worcester, Massachusetts, came up with a game-changing idea: a negotiable order of withdrawal, a NOW account. It worked like a checking account but paid interest on the deposit.

Most people believed it was a joke and would never get off the ground. However, I knew Ron Haseltine and I wasn't so sure. Interest on checking accounts had been prohibited since the passage of the Glass-Steagall Act in 1933 and it was clear if Haseltine was successful he would break the monopoly enjoyed by commercial banks for almost 40 years.

Consumers Savings was insured by the Deposit Insurance Fund of Massachusetts and did not come under FDIC jurisdiction. Haseltine went to the Commissioner of Banks in Massachusetts and instead of asking for permission to offer NOW accounts he took the bold step of announcing what he planned to do.

The Commissioner did not grant approval and sued Consumers to prevent implementation. Haseltine won the lawsuit and a huge political and regulatory uproar followed. It was finally agreed that Massachusetts and New Hampshire banks would be allowed to offer NOW accounts on an experimental basis. The experiment began in 1972 and went national in 1980.

Consumers Savings was not a member of the Fed and needed a vehicle to have the checks honored and cleared on a timely basis. State Street Bank agreed to supply Consumers with checks with the State Street routing number. The checks were cleared through one account number but then had to be sorted by hand at Consumers to the various individual accounts. I talked with one of Haseltine's officers later and he said for a period of time the back office was total chaos. He said they had shoeboxes all over the floor filled with checks that needed to be processed to individual accounts.

I expected vigorous competition as a fact of life, but as long as the experiment stayed in place our expense ratio compared with similar banks in adjoining states would be higher. Although our stock was not actively traded our stock price was a report card on how well management was doing. I thought it would be worthwhile to visit Senator McIntyre and express my concerns, not about competition but about how long the experiment would last. Ed Haseltine who preceded me as President and was Vice Chairman called the senator and arranged a meeting for me at Senator McIntyre's office in Washington.

Senator McIntyre was gracious and listened carefully about my concern involving an uneven playing field if the experiment went on too long. I was surprised he didn't offer any opinions or counter arguments, nor did he mention any thoughts of his Senate colleagues about the ground breaking legislation.

I realized my visit was ill-advised and I was dealing with a savvy politician who was polite but had no interest in what I was saying. As I was leaving he said, "by the way, Rink DeWitt from BankEast was here a few days ago with a similar message and after he left I called the FDIC to see if his bank was in trouble."

When I was leaving he got up from his large desk and put his arm around my shoulder and pointed to some birds outside and said, " those are purple finches. The New Hampshire state bird."

I got back to the office and Haseltine asked me how my meeting with the senator went, I said it was great but we can expect the bank examiners tomorrow. It was a good lesson and I vowed I would never again go to such a meeting without doing more careful homework about the person I was visiting. I should have given the senator material about the subject signed by influential New Hampshire citizens that the Senator would have recognized.

A short while later McIntyre gave a speech which illustrated his total disdain for bankers. He said, "too many in the financial community are sleepy and they are lazy and they are lulled into believing the government will always protect them by regulation and most of all protect them from competition"." The Banking Committee is rarely a forum for the public interest. We regulate primarily for the special interests and what is happening in The Financial Institutions Act is a classic example of what happens when uninformed and uninspired special interests come out of their caves with clubs in hand."

It's difficult not to get really mad when someone calls you sleepy and lazy and a caveman with a club. I didn't think many members of Congress worked long hours and weekends or took much personal risk, but after I calmed down I had to admit Senator McIntyre wasn't entirely wrong.

When I was at the Stonier School of Banking at Rutgers University it was a two year program. We submitted the usual assignments during the two years, but the final hurdle was to submit a thesis and defend your work before a panel of academics and senior bankers.

My paper was based on what I called the three pillars of modern banking.

One: commercial banks had a protected franchise. There were significant requirements to obtain a charter, including sizable paid-in capital. Once all the requirements were met the owners and management knew they would not face unregulated competition.

Two: commercial banks had a very valuable exclusive product franchise, demand deposit checking accounts. Only commercial banks could offer such accounts and interest was prohibited on the account since the passage of the Glass-Steagall Act in1933.

Three: Savings accounts interest rates were controlled by Regulation Q which restricted the interest rates banks could pay. Although thrifts were allowed to pay a slightly higher rate than commercial banks, it did prevent wildcat operations.

Everything was about to change in the days ahead McIntyre said, "how do you deal with an industry that refuses to acknowledge the inevitable."

New Hampshire was booming and we put together several years of very good performance so our stock price was attractive. We decided it was a good time to form a holding company to expand our market.

It proved to be a profitable idea for the share-holders. A number of years later after I had left the bank and was no longer a share-holder, BNH was sold for a large premium.

I decided we didn't need to hire lawyers or consultants to prepare the holding company application for the Federal Reserve Bank as we were not exactly breaking new ground, but I seemed to be running into road blocks at the Fed. Fortunately I made contact with Dan Acquilino, Senior vice President, who never seemed impressed with his position in the Federal Reserve hierarchy. He generously gave me a lot of his time and valuable expertise and knowledge.

The Boston Fed had recently moved from an old office building on Congress Street to a new imposing tower on Atlantic Avenue. Frank Morris, President, had an office that was very grand. Thurber and I met with him for what we assumed was the final hurdle. He sat behind an enormous desk. I tried to see if it was raised somehow because we seemed to be sitting quite a bit lower. Maybe it was a form of intimidation.

After a few minutes a silver tray service arrived with coffee and biscuits. As I recall we were impressed. It turned out to be a very pleasant meeting and we received federal approval shortly afterwards.

The formation of the holding company opened a new chapter with my relationship with Davis Thurber. When a bank becomes part of a holding company management is fundamentally changed, authority and control is assumed by the parent company. I assumed our respective responsibilities would be comparable in the holding company as they were in the bank. Thurber thought otherwise and I was looking at a significant reduction in my authority and responsibilities.

Thurber took an aggressive position and was not open to any negotiations with me or the Executive Committee. Various meetings only inflamed the situation. Thurber invited me to a meeting at his house, although he didn't tell me who would be there my friend and the former president of the bank had alerted me earlier in the day he was having lunch with a lawyer representing the Thurbers. The meeting included Dave and his wife Pat and a well known Boston lawyer. I was not looking for a belligerent meeting but I did ask the lawyer with a smile if I should consider it an ambush. He laughed and proceeded to instruct me on how proxy contests worked. He then went on about the family stock ownership and said they would do whatever was necessary to protect their interests.

I said I thought I had done quite well for all the shareholders. We had maintained a conservative dividend policy while increasing dividends by fifty percent. Per share earnings were up 236 percent in five years, and return on capital was up ninety percent.

At the close of 1980 our loan loss charge off were under one percent. I was hoping for applause but was met with stony silence. It may sound strange but I really enjoyed jousting with their lawyer.

As I was returning to the bank and thinking about our meeting I realized every thing that was happening was at Dave's wife's direction. She did most of the talking at the meeting and made it very clear to me there was no need for more discussion. If necessary they would gain voting control of the stock and replace the Board of Directors and Senior Management.

It was sad. All our hard work was falling apart. Our employees, many of whom were shareholders, were upset and fearful of choosing sides. Our customers were also becoming concerned.

We gave it our best and we had support from all sides, however the probable vote count showed the family owned and controlled a large majority of shares if we went to a proxy contest. I consulted with my closest associates and the non-family members of the Executive Committee and told them I would submit a letter of resignation at the next board meeting. I gave the letter to Davis Thurber, Chairman, and I told him I would not attend the board meeting.

Something highly unlikely happened. The directors apparently ran out of patience and removed Thurber as Chairman. I didn't take any joy in what happened and over the years I wondered if both of us could have done things differently.

I returned to Bank of New Hampshire as Chairman, President and CEO. The titles didn't last long for we lost the proxy contest badly. I didn't make any attempt to influence how any of the officers or employees should vote their shares. They all knew our record and they all had a good idea of the outcome of the voting.

A few days before the vote a woman in the loan department asked to speak to me. She was a very private, quiet person so I was a little surprised. She said she was voting for our side in the proxy fight. I probably should not have done it but I said why don't you hold on to your ballot until the day of the meeting and I will let you know if the vote is close. If it isn't you may want to vote for the other side.

Early in the morning on the final day it was not close and I told her we would lose by a wide margin. She said, "I know, but I'm voting with you!"

I met a lot of great people through the years but none better than my friend in the loan department.

I chaired the final shareholders meeting and after we completed the necessary business, I accepted the resignations of thirteen of fifteen independent directors, including the former President and current Vice Chairman, Ed Hazeltine. It was difficult when the directors wished me good luck and left the meeting.

My friend Bill McGeehan, Executive Vice President and Clerk of the Board, whom I had hired, was removed as clerk and fired. I also was fired by the new CEO, Thurber, and his new Board of Directors.

My wife never wavered during the many months of turmoil and said to me one day, "I would rather eat grass than have you give in just to get a pay-check." She sat through the shareholders meeting with great strength and poise. I shall always be grateful for her love and support.

Organizations generally incur disruptions, expense and loss of momentum during legal battles and proxy contests. BNH was no different but in time the bank recovered. BNH was sold to a Maine bank which in turn sold to Toronto Dominion Bank in Canada. Bank of New Hampshire continues today as TD Bank. I'm one of their loyal customers in Peterborough, New Hampshire.

Chapter 8

Interlude

After I left Bank of New Hampshire I thought it would be a good idea to get back into the game as soon as possible. I did the usual networking and had several interviews for positions that were comparable to the one I had. I knew there were not many perfect jobs, but I think I was being overly cautious about making another mistake.

Although I was happy to stand on my record and fortunately I had excellent references from my directors, customers and even competitors, it was inevitable I would have to discuss why I was fired, which involved personalities and that was difficult.

I eventually decided it was a good time to use my experience, good and bad, and go it alone as a bank consultant. The mutual savings banks in New England were converting or considering converting from mutual ownership to public stock ownership. Many small to medium size commercial banks were thinking about mergers or buyouts by a holding company. I thought my experience would have some value.

I was retained by Amoskeag Savings Bank, the largest bank in New Hampshire which had converted to stock ownership and was receiving pressure to increase earnings. I worked with them on changing their culture from home mortgage lending to a more full service bank.

Concord Saving Bank was in the evaluation stage of converting and I worked with a group of officers and trustees in making the decision.

I also worked with a Vermont Bank that was considering joining another Vermont Bank to form a holding company to own both banks.

In addition to my bank consulting business a former associate whom I hired at State Street had gone in the executive search business and asked me to join him as president of the business. We both had very good contacts with New England bankers and it was a good opportunity for me to do both consulting and search.

Although I did some successful searches, in time I decided I should concentrate on bank consulting.

Shortly after we ended our amicable association my friend called and said he had received a call from an executive at State Street Bank who asked him to approach me about returning to run the retail business. Although it might have been interesting to return for a meeting to discuss what they had in mind, I declined because it seemed obvious to me they were still moving away from retail business.

My friend called again and said Multibank, which was a Massachusetts holding company was looking for a president for their bank in Fall River. I appreciated his call but did not follow up with a meeting. A few days later he called and said, "You said no too quickly. You have to meet with Sel Atherton, the President of Multibank, and this is a really good situation."

My friend didn't give up easily. I knew Sel Atherton from my correspondent banking days when he was president of a bank in Lewiston, Maine. Atherton was a very smart and savvy banker. I had a very good meeting with him and subsequently met with the chairman of Multibank and the Fall River directors.

I decided to give up my consulting business and join Durfee-Attleborough Bank as their new president. I said earlier some of the best people I ever met in my life were off the beaten path in Maine. I very quickly added hundreds more in Fall River and Bristol County.

A few years later a decision was made to merge Durfee-Attleborough Bank and Falmouth National Bank on Cape Cod with South Shore Bank, the holding companies flagship bank in Quincy. I went along as president of the new South Shore Bank.

Chapter 9

Murder, Threats And Protests

One of my early assignments at State Street was to make arrangements for the annual meeting at a Boston hotel. It was a routine sort of thing until I received a call from a highly agitated guy who kept repeating he was coming to the meeting to kill me along with my pig friends.

I decided not to hang up abruptly so I might get his name or location but his language just became more violent. We had a good contact at the Boston Police Department and the Agent in Charge of the Boston FBI office both said they did not have any information.

It was an uneventful meeting, however death threats and protests were to become part of banking life.

It's not generally known that there isn't a lot of cash in a bank branch and not a great deal more in the main vault. I was named person to take care of the banking needs of the Saudi royal family when the Saudi King came to Boston for surgery. Chase Bank asked us to provide whatever the royal family needed, including large amounts of cash.

The entourage took over two floors at a Boston hotel and every day a Saudi Prince arrived with a driver and took away a suitcase loaded with tens of thousands of dollars of cash. It was a wild scene for a while at many of the nightspots.

On a more serious note regarding the availability of large amounts of cash on short notice, during the Vietnam War era there was concern about having enough cash in the event of a hostage taking. State Street and other banks, including the Boston Federal Reserve Bank did not have any vaults open during the weekends. I made arrangements with Chase, which had a large vault open seven days a week to obtain funds if needed.

Although any well-known person would have been a target, several of us believed that Dick Hill, President of the First National Bank of Boston, was a high risk target.

Fortunately a hostage situation never happened, but the murder of a Boston police officer by a group of anti-Vietnam War protesters happened in 1970. It was the most violent and tragic of robberies and happened at the State Street branch in Brighton.

The State Street Bank branch office in Brighton was a new stand alone office in a mixed residential/business area not far from Harvard Business School. It didn't seem like the kind of place for a shootout and murder.

In September 1970 the branch was robbed by three men and two women who were armed with an automatic rifle, a shotgun, handguns and a knife. It was later learned the same group had robbed the National Guard Armory in Newburyport a few days earlier and had stolen guns, and 400 rounds of ammunition before setting fire to the building causing $125,000 in damages.

The robbers burst into the Brighton office shouting obscenities and firing shots above the employees heads into the walls and ceiling. William Levin was a recent college graduate who had taken a summer job as a teller. He was directed at knifepoint to fill a canvas bag with all the money from the teller cash drawers. Bill Levin managed to include marked bills. Bank robbers generally were aware of exploding dye packs and marked bills and often warned tellers that if they included either the dye pack or the marked bills they would be killed.

The robbers included William "Lefty" Gilday, Stanley Bond, Robert Valeri, Susan Saxe and Katherine Ann Power. When Officer William Schroeder answered the alarm he was unaware the robbers had left the building and were in their cars. As Officer Schroeder was entering the building Gilday shot him in the back with automatic rifle fire. Schroeder was no immediate threat to them and they could have driven away, however, they chose to murder the police officer.

After shooting Schroeder, Gilday sprayed the windows and façade of the bank with gunfire. Although they claimed to be protesting the Vietnam War they made a neighborhood bank look like a bombed out war zone.

Officer Schroeder died in the hospital the next day. He left his wife and nine children. The youngest was only seven months old. Mrs. Schroeder asked her oldest daughter Claire, to tell her brothers and sisters that their father had died.

Katherine Power and Susan Saxe were roommates at Brandeis University. Power is an interesting study. She was a native of Denver, Colorado. She made disparaging remarks about her provincial upbringing, but her father was a bank credit manager and her mother was a registered nurse. She won a scholarship to Marycrest Girls High School, a Catholic school, and she was the valedictorian of her class.

Power became romantically involved with Stanley Bond, an ex-soldier who was taking special courses at Brandeis. Power, Saxe and Bond were active in the National Student Strike Force which helped organize anti-Vietnam War protests around the country. When she attended the Brandeis class Reunion in June, 2012 she recalled her days in the Pearlman Lounge, the long-ago site where the National Student Strike Force held meetings.

Bond introduced Power and Saxe to William "Lefty" Gilday, a former convict, and Robert Valeri. Although Power helped plan the bank robbery and drove one of the getaway cars, she later referred to Gilday and Valeri as two thugs.

The three men were arrested shortly after the robbery and murder of Walter Schroeder. All three were given lengthy prison sentences. Gilday got life and Valeri testified against Gilday and was given a 25 year sentence and is now free. Bond came to a violent end and blew himself up trying to make a bomb and escape jail.

Power and Saxe escaped and lived in various communes before separating. Saxe was arrested five years later in 1975 and served five years in prison and is also now free.

Power was one of the few females on the FBI's most wanted list. The FBI received virtually no information about her whereabouts and she was dropped from the list in 1984. For twenty-three years she managed to stay in hiding in Oregon. She got married and raised a son before surrendering to Massachusetts authorities in 1993. She served six years for the robbery and shooting of Officer Schroeder and was granted parole in 1999.

Because I was personally familiar with the robbery and murder, I read about her parole. Although I thought six years was a short time to serve for what she had done her verbal apology to the Schroeder family seemed sincere. The life she lived after the robbery and her conduct in prison seemed exemplary. I assumed there was no need to write anything more about the tragic story.

I was surprised, however, to read an opinion piece in the "Boston Herald" newspaper in May, 2012 written by William Levin. The title was, "A Victim Rebuts Power." it was the same Bill Levin who was held at knife point during the State Street Bank robbery in 1970. Levin is a professor emeritus at Centre College in Kentucky.

It was a wonderful experience to have a long telephone conversation with Bill Levin. As he was recounting the story of the robbery and the hail of gunfire before and after the robbery and later learning that Officer Schroeder had died, I could tell he was reliving the whole episode. He told me of another tragedy he and his wife had experienced. Their 20-year-old daughter was killed by random gunfire when visiting her 90 year old aunt in Roxbury.

Bill Levin is a remarkable person in spite of all he has endured. I did not hear bitterness or a refusal to forgive Katherine Power if she truly regretted her actions during her college days, however, he found the essay she wrote for the Brandeis magazine in 2012 expressing regret for her actions not wholly believable. He referred me to a PBS documentary which I had not seen.

The documentary is a disturbing reminder of the anti-Vietnam War protest and how badly our country was torn apart. I believe in redemption and forgiving, as Bill Levin does but after reading Ms. Power's essay and reviewing the documentary, I believe that Professor Levin was right. I cannot except her claim that she really regrets her anti war days at Brandeis.

She wrote, "I was ashamed and embarrassed by the recklessness and ingratitude I had shown Brandeis University that had been so generous to me, that opened the gate to my provincial Catholic ghetto and shown me the world."

The world she was speaking about was one of violence and murder. Walter Schroeder's daughter spoke at Power's parole hearing and said, "Murdering the policeman to bring peace in South East Asia was utterly senseless then and it is just as senseless now."

People like Bill Ayers and Katherine Power seem to believe it was their duty to injure and even murder to bring about change rather than use their considerable intellect and privilege to persuade others to their cause.

It was a dark period in history and should be a warning that a country that is badly divided can have terrible trouble.

Several years after the Brighton robbery, when I was head of the retail division at State Street Bank, we had repeated robberies at our Dudley

Street office in Roxbury. It was a high crime area, so much so that we had to have an armed guards escort our employees to the parking area behind the building.

My boss said, "you have a good relationship with the bank commissioner. Why don't you ask her for permission to close the office."

I visited with the commissioner and briefly made my case I also referred to the prior robbery and shooting in Brighton.

She said, "well no one was hurt in the recent robbery but do whatever you think is right." I hadn't expected such an easy approval so I thanked her and headed for the door; she then said, "by the way don't ever ask this office for anything again and be sure to tell your boss George Rockwell the same."

Rockwell asked how the meeting went and I said I don't think it's a good idea to close Dudley Street. He said it's a sign of things to come and he was right, the Community Reinvestment Act was just around the corner.

During my many years in banking we had regular robberies at our branch offices. An unusual exception was a robbery at the main office of Bank of New Hampshire. Two robbers entered the bank during the busiest part of the day. One was completely out-of-control and dangerous.

As they were running from the building, the violent robber's bag of stolen funds caught on the door handle and ripped open and all of the stolen funds were recovered on the sidewalk. I assume his partner was not too happy.

Although it's rare for a bank employee to be hurt during a robbery I always had in mind the State Street robbery. We advised employees to cooperate and not try any heroics. If you talk to an employee who has had a gun pointed at his or her head by a robber who appears high on drugs or alcohol you will hear about how traumatic the experience is.

Chapter 10

Demonstrations And Pickets

I was President of Durfee Attleboro Bank in Fall River in December 1983 when I received a call from the mayors office alerting me of the possibility of a demonstration by a group of disgruntled workers employed by one of our customers.

If the name of the bank sounds a little odd imagine the original name, before the merger with the Attleboro Trust Company. It was the B.M.C. Durfee Trust. The owners of the bank had named it after their son, Bradford Matthew Chalnor Durfee.

I guess if you are J. P. Morgan and name the bank after yourself it will work out okay, however, if you are in Fall River and want more than a handful of customers, naming the bank after your son it's not good marketing.

Although the bank name had been changed, it was still known by many as the "mill owners bank." We spent years trying to earn the trust of the whole community. Fall River has a large immigrant population from the Azores and at one time was a large textile manufacturing city.

Two weeks before Christmas one of our customers, a fireplace equipment manufacturer, closed down in the middle of the night and fled. We were owed a modest amount of money, but some 30 employees were owed two weeks wages and some overtime.

Fortunately I was able to meet with a committee of three of the employees before a demonstration was scheduled. I was expecting a difficult meeting but had not decided what we would do. I was surprised they did not make any demands or threaten to have pickets outside my office the next day. They simply said we did not get paid for our work and we need help.

I thought we make charitable contributions to various community organizations, why not do something that has an immediate impact that helps a lot of families? I agreed to pay the employees wages our customer had cheated them out of. I understood it was not my money but I never had a shareholder complain when their company did the right thing . We made a lot of new friends in Fall River two weeks before Christmas.

This one time, I was referred to by a talk show host as Santa Claus!

After moving to South Shore bank in Quincy in 1986, I was not as fortunate as I was at Durfee Attleboro Bank in avoiding a major demonstration. I received a call that one of our customers, a mental health agency, had abruptly closed it's doors. Apparently no one saw it coming so there were many clients without services and a large number of professionals and employees who were owed salaries.

The agency had a payroll account with us but did not have a borrowing relationship so there was no reason for us to be knowledgeable about the agency's financial affairs. The problem was mismanagement by the executive director. She was not guilty of wrongdoing but the agency was in debt and insolvent.

Unfortunately the directors, their financial officer, and their independent auditor, and the Commonwealth of Massachusetts did not raise any warning flags before the collapse. I was told that the Director of Health and Human Services for Massachusetts had assured everyone that South Shore Bank would pay all wages. My calls to him were never answered.

I was given the name of the spokesperson for the group that was organizing a demonstration at our bank I called her and asked her if she and her group, hopefully not more than a dozen people, would meet with me at the bank. She and a large group of very hostile people showed up.

I introduced myself and my long-time friend and colleague, Jack McNamara, whose daughter was a client of the agency. Before I could say much else, the spokesperson kept yelling, "we're not here to listen to excuses. Either agree to pay us right now or we will be back tomorrow with hundreds of pickets and close your bank down."

There was a lot of yelling and stomping of feet and the whole thing ended in chaos.

Early the next day a large group of pickets showed up, the media also arrived in full force. I noticed an athletic looking young guy on crutches limping around the picket line, his face etched in pain. The health professionals knew how to make me look heartless.

We had nothing to do with the failure of the agency but it's impossible to have any reasonable dialogue with people screaming terrible epithets. After a long period the protesters began to run out of steam and the TV crews were packing up, when one of the organizers grabbed a bullhorn and started whipping things up again. The TV crews came back to life.

Everything eventually quieted down. It was a long unpleasant day, but the next one was going to be even more personally punishing.

We had an armed robbery at one of our branch offices in Wellesley, in September 1990. It's a federal crime to rob a bank with FDIC insurance and generally the amount taken is relatively small considering the risk. The amount the robbers got was $1800.

It was another robbery in which one of the gunmen appeared high on drugs and threatened everyone with vulgar threats and demands. One employee was in the lunch room and heard what was happening and called 911. She had forgotten that the extension light would go on at the teller stations.

One of her colleagues told me she was looking at the barrel of a gun close to her face and out of the corner of her eye she saw the light go on. She said she began praying that the crazed robber would not see it. Fortunately he did not!

She visited me later and said she was seeing a doctor because she was having nightmares and trouble sleeping. She had been with us for a number of years and loved all the people she worked with and would miss "her customers" but she couldn't take it anymore and had to retire. I understood but it was very sad to lose such a good person.

A few days later I got a call from our Wellesley Hills office manager who sounded panicky. I asked if someone was hurt. She said no, but we have a problem. She said she saw a black male across the street and she was sure it was the same person who had robbed the bank. Another employee agreed.

She said she had called the police and they had responded with several police cars and seven or more cops came with guns drawn. The suspect had entered a Mercedes with a woman but was ordered out and handcuffed face-down on the sidewalk. His friend was screaming that he was not a bank robber. He was a basketball player with the Boston Celtics.

The police quickly realized their mistake and apologized to the man and the woman. The Wellesley police were in for a rough time but not anything like we were.

The person mistakenly arrested was Dee Brown, a top draft choice with the Celtics. Brown and his fiancée, Jill Edmondson, were considering buying a house in Wellesley and were picking up mail at the post office.

I immediately called the Celtics office to see if I could arrange a meeting to apologize to their new player in person. It was apparent they didn't want me to show up at the Boston Garden, but they gave me a telephone number where I could reach Mr. Brown. I tried a number of times but was not able to reach him

It didn't take long for things to career out of control. The Boston newspapers, TV and radio stations and local media went ballistic. South Shore Bank was labeled a hotbed of racism and I was the head racist. A talk show host in Boston spent one whole program encouraging everyone to boycott the bank and he kept referring to me as an ignorant racist. We were getting badly pummeled.

This time I received death threats and a blizzard of hate mail. One mailing was a drawing of our house with flames coming out of the roof and another was a rather good picture of the bank building with crosshairs placed on my office window.

A group in Wellesley formed the Wellesley–African American Citizen Committee. Their agenda called for improved communication with the Wellesley police and town officials. The selectmen announced an open town meeting with the committee and the towns people. I asked if I could attend the meeting and they agreed but I was told I was not on the program of speakers.

It was a constructive and very polite meeting, without heated rhetoric or blame. The moderator eventually asked me if I would like to say a few words.

I was careful not to make any excuses for our mistake. I said I wanted to express my apologies to Dee Brown and Jill Edmondson, the Wellesley police and all the people in Wellesley.

As President of South Shore Bank no one who worked with me could say that I ever used inappropriate or racial language. I also said we had hundreds of employees and I didn't know what was in each person's heart, but as a company we did not tolerate discrimination or racism.

I said we had emphasized the need to be extremely careful about making an identification and we would initiate in-house seminars to address ethnic and racial issues in the workplace.

In time life returned to normal, as most people agreed we were not an Evil Empire.

I didn't ask anyone to accompany me to the Wellesley meeting, however Fred Healy a Senior Vice President and loyal friend insisted on going with me. He said he understood we might be stoned to death.

Chapter 11

Saul Alinsky

I had an office on Tremont Street in Boston when I was head of the BankAmericard Department at State Street Bank. The office was on the second floor of an old Boston building and I could see part of the plaza in front of City Hall. The plaza is huge and was the perfect place to stage anti-VietnamWar protests. Regular large demonstrations happened until it turned cold and started snowing.

My wife and I had lived in Boston before I went into the army for a brief tour and when we came back we again lived there for a short period. Boston is an absolutely lovely city and it was shocking to see large groups of riot police with helmets, shields and batons and armored cars on a side street in the event things got out of hand.

I often went out to talk to some of the demonstrators. Many were young from area colleges, enjoying a day off, but they also were very serious about their opposition to the war. I mentioned to several that when I was a senior in high school I signed up for the draft during the Korean War on my 18th birthday. The response was always the same - even if it was the law they would not have signed up for the draft.

Tom Hayden, when he was active with Abbie Hoffman and Jerry Ruben in the Students for a Democratic Society said, "if you can get a middle class person to break the law you were well on the way to creating a revolutionary."

I have read both of Saul Alinsky's books, "Reveille for Radicals" and "Rules for Radicals." If I had read them much earlier in my career I would have been better prepared for the demonstrations I faced. Alinsky's tactics are still being used in current demonstrations.

Hillary Clinton wrote her senior thesis at Wellesley College on Alinsky's theories. Ms. Rodman's work indicated she knew the stated issue of a protest such as poverty or discrimination was not the real issue – the real issue was about gaining power and ultimate need for power was for revolution. It did not need to be bloody but it did mean dramatic change.

Hillary Rodman interviewed Saul Alinsky for her work and after she graduated from Wellesley Alinsky offered her a position at his Training Institute. As we know she opted for Yale Law school instead.

Alinsky began his career as a community organizer in Chicago and developed his playbook for organizing mass demonstrations during the Depression.

He was not the typical radical. He dressed like the bankers he hated, had short hair and big glasses. He had little regard for LBJ's Great Society. He considered handouts had little effect on the problems. He wanted dramatic changes.

He organized his first protest in an area of Chicago known as "Back of theYards" near the meat packing district. He described the area as defeated, without hope and with no leadership. The area had a terrible problem of infant mortality.

He learned that a number of years earlier the Infant Welfare Society had operated clinics in the neighborhood but the churches called the clinics, " agents of sin" because they distributed birth-control information. The churches forced the clinics to close.

Alinsky found the clinics would return as soon as asked, but he did not tell his followers. He organized a meeting to storm the agency and told his followers if anyone from the agency tried to speak they should be shouted down. When the woman tried to say they would be pleased to return, every time she tried to speak, he yelled "is it yes or no?"

The clinics returned and he had an easy victory; his next attempt, however, was a failure. He tried to organize the meatpackers but found they did not have a high level of concern about their public image. He decided to target the banks where they had their accounts. He was right. The bankers complained to the meatpackers.

Alinsky had hundreds of volunteers descend on the designated bank and open savings accounts for a few dollars or engage in other time-consuming transactions. He was able to prevent most of the regular customers from even getting inside the bank.

He used the tactic many times, sometimes with more than 1000 volunteers. It became known as a "bank in." A similar tactic called a "shop in" was used to shut down retail outlets.

Jesse Jackson learned a lot about demonstrations from Alinsky. He literally shut down O'Hare International Airport by having hundreds of his followers overwhelm the restrooms. Steel workers in Pittsburgh added some nasty touches such as spraying a bank building with some skunk oil or putting dead fish in safe deposit boxes.

Alinsky also used skillful psychological tactics in his demonstrations. In 1972 George H. W. Bush was the U. S. Ambassador to the United Nations and was scheduled to speak at Tulane University. A group of students planned to protest and asked Alinsky for advice.

They were surprised when he told them their plan of shouting and yelling to interrupt Bush's speech was the wrong approach. He advised them to dress as Ku Klux Klan members and carry KKK signs and every time Bush said something positive about the Vietnamwar they should stand up and yell, "the KKK supports Bush."

The media coverage was everything the students hoped for.

Chapter 12

Multibank Financial Corporation

Multibank Financial Corporation was a small Massachusetts holding company. In the late 1980s it was decided to combine several of the smaller banks into larger ones. The bank in Springfield was combined with the bank in Pittsfield to form Multibank West and my bank, Durfee Attleboro, was merged with Falmouth National on the Cape with South Shore bank in Quincy. I went along with the merger as president of South Shore Bank. The third bank in the holding company was Mechanics Bank in Worcester.

South Shore was a wonderful old institution that was formed more than 150 years ago at Fowels Tavern in Quincy. Although Quincy is only a few miles from Boston in the early days the stage to Boston ran once a day, leaving at 8:30 AM and returning at 4 PM.

Farmers and merchants found it inconvenient to take a whole day off to transact banking business. There was growing sentiment for a group to petition the Massachusetts legislature for a charter for a hometown bank.

The group was able to raise $100,000 for capital from individuals in all parts of the community. It was an impressive amount at the time and in March 1836 the legislature via special act incorporated the Quincy Stone Bank. It was the first bank in the United States to raise all its capital funds by public subscription. John Quincy Adams was among the investors.

The early years were difficult. The failure of the Second Bank of the United States and the panic of 1837 caused many banks to fail. Quincy Stone Bank, as solid as its name, survived and weathered the storm.

Commercial banks in our early days were either prohibited from making real estate mortgages or simply refused to do so. The president of the bank and several colleagues formed the Quincy Savings Bank to fill the need.

Josiah Brigham, the second president of Quincy Stone Bank, also served as president of Quincy Savings Bank for almost 10 years. Eventually legislation required the separation of commercial banking and savings banking by prohibiting interlocking officers and directors. I'm happy to say, however, even when I was in Quincy we enjoyed a good relationship with Chuck Simpson at Quincy Savings and worked together on a number of community projects.

The Civil War brought great hardship and loss of life in the South and the North. Congress passed the National Bank Act of 1864 which levied a 10% tax on state bank issued notes. In a short period of time almost all state banks converted to national charters, including Quincy Stone Bank which became the National Granite Bank.

The state banks that refused to be taxed into allegiance with the federal government changed from issuing their own paper to deposit banking, which in time proved so advantageous most banks converted.

Theophilus King was elected president of the bank in 1886. When he was elected he owned 10 qualifying shares, 25 years later he owned all the shares except qualifying director shares.

Throughout the 1920s the economy was booming and Quincy and the surrounding areas were participating. Mr. King decided it was a good time to build a new impressive bank building. The new building was opened in 1929, not a good year, but in spite of the stock market crash and Great Depression the bank survived and remained a major financial presence in Quincy.

Many of the Art Deco buildings of the time have been torn down to make room for more modern structures, but the old bank building at the top of the Square in Quincy still seems to me it's everything Mr. King wanted to convey. It's an image of strength and permanence.

Robert Campbell wrote in the Boston Globe at the time of the banks 150th anniversary in 1990, "South Shore's chief glory is the interior banking hall, a space with enough grandeur to convince any customer of the banks wealth and stability."

"The Hall is spanned by a delicate shallow vaulted skylight and it's walls - which appear to be made of limestone - are lined with pilasters whose tops step back like the top of the building itself."

"Brass trim chandeliers, carved wood teller stations, inlaid marble floors and lovely brass writing desks complete a fine interior."

I was told that the main entrance, which is four massive columns of dark polished Quincy granite, are the largest single pieces ever carved by the skilled stone masons of the day.

I was talking with Tony Larsordo, a former director and long-time customer one day and I asked him about the construction of the bank. We went down to the banking floor and examined the columns. Tony explained they were travertine, made from a mixture of stone dust and cement (probably calcium carbonate). After all the years the columns were as perfect as the day they were put in place.

It was from another time and I loved it. The last time I walked through the banking hall, I thought how fortunate I was to have been even a small part of the history of South Shore Bank which soon would become just another branch bank.

Mr. King and his family were very generous supporters of their church in their community during their lifetimes; even to this day, two charitable trusts continue to make contributions as directed by Mr. and Mrs. King.

I had the honor to chair the King family trust for a number of years. Our instructions were to make annual donations to every church and synagogue in Quincy. Mr. King said, "to help and bear the strongest testimony of which I am capable… Through the breaking down of prejudices and better understanding of each other's religious faith."

In later years we found more than 50 churches, two synagogues, and one Muslim mosque that qualified for contributions. Some were small and held services in rented or donated spaces. Every year I visited with several. One year I was curious that one church listed two addresses for the same building. I asked some friends if they knew about the church and I was assured it was an active church with a great pastor. They were right. I had a wonderful visit with the pastor and found he had two congregations, one meeting in the morning and the other in the afternoon. He told me Mr. King's donation meant a lot to his churches. I think Mr. King would be happy we were carrying out his wishes just as he wanted.

I told my directors every time I looked out my window at the Boston skyline I was sure someone at Bank of Boston was looking at us through a telescope. We all knew it was only a matter of time before the restrictions on branches and mergers would be removed and South Shore Bank would be a major target of Bank of Boston.

The First National Bank of Boston came very close to acquiring Granite Trust, (our name at the time) in 1956. A federal law was passed that allowed a national bank in Massachusetts to extend its operations up to 15 miles from the home office.

The law was so narrowly drawn and specific to Massachusetts it was reasonable to assume First National Bank had something to do with the law. Immediately after it was passed executives from First National Bank approached the Granite Bank directors with a consolidation plan.

The Granite directors were not enthusiastic, however they believed the competitive landscape had been dramatically changed and they recommended the consolidation plan to the shareholders. To facilitate the plan the bank converted to a national charter and became Granite National Bank of Quincy.

Although it looked like the deal was done, a political uproar erupted. Charles Howard, Bank Commissioner, vigorously opposed the merger, saying it would end dual banking in the Commonwealth.

Senator John Kennedy spoke out strongly against the plan and urged the Comptroller of the Currency to delay approval until the legislature could review the matter. Governor Foster Furcolo persuaded the legislature to pass a temporary bill blocking the merger. Both sides decided to end the talks on an amicable basis and the Comptroller of the Currency withdrew his approval. The Granite directors changed the bank name to South Shore Bank.

The South Shore area began a period of rapid expansion beginning in the early 1950s. The construction of Route 128, Route 3 and the Southeast Expressway tied the area together and improved access to Boston. The population and the economy were growing rapidly.

The South Shore board of directors decided it was the right time to embark on an aggressive expansion plan. In 1968, they formed a one bank holding company called Shore Bank, the first of its kind in Massachusetts. The Shore Bank executives were very aggressive in expanding not only traditional banking but in going well outside the "normal" banking activities. They drove the people at the Federal Reserve Bank of Boston absolutely crazy.

At various times Shore Bank owned a check printing company, a discount brokerage company, a travel agency, and Multibank International. Eventually the Feds prevailed and the above companies,with the exception of Multibank International, were abandoned or sold.

During my time at the bank, I was president of Multibank International and we also had an active business financing small aircraft. We had two licensed pilots, a company plane, and an office at the Mansfield airport.

South Shore Bank was in a great position to expand in Norfolk County, the bank acquired Weymouth Trust Company, Randolph Trust Company, National Bank of Wareham, Norwood Bank and Trust and Wellesley Trust.

In 1992 Shore Bank Holding Company was reorganized to form Multibank Financial Corporation.

The inevitable happened in 1993. Bank of Boston acquired Multibank and I became a Regional President with virtually no responsibility except not to speak negatively about the merger.

My opposition to the acquisition did not win me many friends in Boston but once the deal was done I accepted the fact I should either join the new team or leave. After a brief period, I decided it had been a good run but it was time to leave. My opposition admittedly was personal but South Shore Bank was doing well and it seemed to me the acquisition price would be substantially higher in two years or less.

Chapter 13

The Fed Goes Rogue

The last Massachusetts Bankers Association meeting I attended in 1993 was at the Sheraton Tara in Framingham. The program looked interesting but hardly groundbreaking. Alicia Munnell, a Senior Vice President and Director of Research at the Federal Reserve Bank of Boston, was the lead speaker.

Before she spoke I noticed Richard Syron, President of the Fed, standing in the front of the room where he carefully surveyed the audience several times. He remained there as she spoke, nodding approval. It seemed an odd and unnecessary display of support for one of his senior officers who should have been comfortable speaking to a group of bankers.

I learned later that Ms. Munnell and Lynne Browne authored a study of mortgage lending in late 1992 titled, "Mortgage Lending in Boston: Interpreting HMDA Data." The study was published in 1993.

The title was bland enough, but the conclusions were incendiary. The study charged area lenders with pervasive discrimination. As an area lender the charge struck a raw nerve.

The study was followed in six months with a manual called, "Closing the Gap" which laid out a road map for bankers to correct the charge of discrimination in lending and their failure to meet the needs in underserved communities.

Richard Syron had an impressive academic background with a degree in economics. He like to be introduced as Dr. Syron. Syron introduced the Fed study saying, "This comports completely with common sense and I don't think you need a lot more studies like this."

Alicia Munnell joined in and said without any apparent concern for academic modesty, "This study eliminates all other possible factors that could be influencing mortgage decisions."[1]

Ms. Munnell left the Fed shortly after the study was published and later said she had no part in writing the manual. She joined Robert Rubin at the Treasury as an Assistant Secretary and currently is a professor at Boston College.

I believe Richard Syron was using his position as President of the prestigious Boston Fed to promote himself as the person to totally change the way mortgage lending was done in this country even if that meant browbeating, bankers into demolishing their traditional underwriting standards.

Although there were early critics of the methodology used in the study, Syron arrogantly refused to listen. Alicia Munnell agreed that there were flaws that the critics raised, but she stood by the conclusions.

The study was based on data supplied by lenders in accordance with the Home Mortgage Disclosure act (HMDA) 1975, which was signed by President Gerald Ford. It simply required lenders to disclose lending patterns. In 1991, President George H.W. Bush signed an amended HMDA which required lenders to provide data so comparisons could be made of rejection rates by race.

Unfortunately the law did not provide essential data for discrimination based on race and legitimate considerations based on creditworthiness such as the applicant's income.

I think most of us would agree that if the methodology used in a study is seriously flawed one should be cautious about using the conclusion. In spite of the early warning signs from recognized academics, the Boston Study set off a firestorm in the mortgage industry.

The Fed Study was embraced by the Clinton administration, members of Congress, bank regulators and many economists and it created a long period of damage before it was realized the study was unreliable.

Several years after the study was published the Federal Reserve Board of Governors in Washington published a report in December 1996 which essentially withdrew its support. The governors chose their words carefully and said, "the data have important limitations... and care must be taken in drawing conclusions from observed lending patterns. Foremost among these limitations is a lack of information about factors that are important in determining the credit worthiness of applicants and the adequacy of the collateral offered."[2]

It was a stunning rebuke, but several years too late. Janet Reno, Atty. General, Andrew Como, Secretary of Housing (HUD), congressional representatives, federal regulators and the media accepted without question that racial discrimination existed in mortgage lending.

The Boston Fed Study and the Community Reinvestment Act and the Fair Housing Act were used by the Clinton team to impose quotas on mortgage lenders which I will comment on in more detail under Community Reinvestment Act chapter fourteen.

Because the Boston Study labeled me and other area bankers racists I would like to comment in further detail. Sometimes you have to be the target of an unfair claim by the Feds to experience the full effect of the power of the US government.

First I would like to cite several other recommendations from the Closing the Gap Manual which I believe demonstrates a complete misunderstanding about how business operates.

"The board should consider working with other lenders either to establish a buyer education program to provide financial resources so that community services agencies can set up a program."

It is not clear whether the directors should take such action, independent of management, or does it mean the board should direct management to set up such a program?

It is not a workable recommendation and it is unlikely we or any other bank would allocate funds to ACORN or any other group to tell us how to run our business.

Another recommendation was, "Financial institutions may wish to organize and participate in multibank mortgage review boards." It is a little like the old saying, "Does Macys tell Gimbels?" I am sure the mortgage people from Bank of Boston would like to tell us how to run our mortgage company.

The final recommendation I found really repugnant, "The Board can work with management to determine the feasibility of using shoppers to test for discrimination in the pre-application stage."

I never considered spying on my associates as an option and I would not work for a company engaged in such activities.

I could continue at length but will close with the recommendation which basically advised us to get unrealistic property appraisals in low income neighborhoods.

"Management should be aware that Fannie Mae and Freddie Mac have issued statements to the effect that they understand urban areas require different appraisal methods. Accordingly it may be an advantage to use the services of appraisers with experience in conducting appraisals in minority and low income neighborhoods. Management should consider having all appraisal reports that would cause an application to be denied being reviewed by another experienced appraiser. This can help protect the financial institution as well, as it may be held liable if an appraisal is found to be discriminatory."

Syron's introduction to "Closing the Gap Manuel" said "they had gathered recommendations on best practices from lending institutions and consumer groups."

I was still in banking when the Study and Manual were published and we owned a good-sized mortgage company in the metropolitan Boston area. I did not receive either publication nor did any of my associates, including Judy Pfeffer who ran our mortgage company.

Judy Pfeffer also served on the Massachusetts Bankers Association Mortgage Committee and it was well-known that she and her associates had initiated an outreach program to the large Asian immigrant population in Quincy that provided loan counseling and instruction and mortgage terminology.

My successor who was a regional President for Bank of Boston subsequently told me that the Study and Manual were never mentioned in any Bank of Boston meetings or in memoranda.

Professor Stan J. Lebowitz, Professor of Economics at the University of Texas was one of the earliest critics of the Boston study. He wrote a lengthy article, "Anatomy of a Train Wreck, The Causes of the Mortgage Meltdown" in the National Review, October 20, 2008.

Liebowitz wrote, "the Boston Fed collected data on approximately 3000 mortgages. Data problems were obvious to anyone who bothered to examine the numbers. The loan data had information that implied, if it were to be believed, that hundreds of loans had interest rates that were much too high or much too low. "About 50 loans had negative interest rates, over 500 applications could not be matched to the original HMDA upon which the Boston data was supposedly based."

"Forty-four loans were supposedly rejected by the lender, but then sold in the secondary market, which is impossible. Over 500 loans were approved in spite of no evidence of insurance."

"Several mortgages were supposedly approved for individuals with net worth in the negative millions of dollars."

Such shoddy, unreliable work suggests a rush to get something published which was unworthy of the prestigious Boston Fed.

David Horne, an economist with the FDIC wrote in Financial Services Research in November 1997, that he found similar problems. He found that relevant credit history was lacking in many of the denials. Interestingly he found that 49 of 70 banks had not rejected any minority loan applicants and two of the remaining 21 responsible for more than half of the denials of black applicants, one had an extensive minority outreach program.[3]

Nobel Laureate Gary Becker, who pioneered the study of discrimination economics stated the study had enormous problems. "The flaw in all studies of discrimination by banks in application mortgages is that they have not determined the profitability of different groups.... a valid study of discrimination would calculate default rates, late payments, interest rates and other determinates of the profitability of loans."[4] Prof. Leibowitz invited the Boston Fed Group, to participate in a seminar he was giving at the Dallas Fed (note the venue). They spoke for 45 minutes but unlike Leibowitz they refused to take questions saying they had to catch a plane. They also claimed they had new data, however never produced it.

It was an unusual lack of courtesy and academic courage by the Boston Fed group.

Chapter 14

The Community Reinvestment Act (CRA)

The Community Reinvestment Act (CRA) of 1977 was signed into law by President Jimmy Carter. It was designed to "encourage" bankers to meet the needs of borrowers in all segments of the community where they did business.

The law was clear in the beginning as it stated that an institution's "compliance activities should be undertaken in a safe and sound manner."

It had little enforcement provisions and examination of a bank's compliance with the law was generally left to the examiner in charge. I would like to comment on my personal experience with a CRA exam and how it was later strengthened during the Clinton administration.

It was late in the game for me when the Community Reinvestment Act (CRA) examiner arrived to do a compliance examination of our mortgage company.

Multibank Mortgage Company was jointly owned by South Shore Bank 50 percent, Mechanics Bank in Worcester 25 percent, and Multibank West in Pittsfield 25 percent. The company was headquartered at South Shore Bank. Judy Pfeffer ran the company and was a vice president of the bank. We shared management and financial responsibility with the holding company but a CRA exam was directed almost wholly at South Shore Bank.

The first day the examiner was with us we ran into an unexpected problem; we had recently elected to become a smoke-free building and the examiner was a chain-smoker. Although we gave her a private office in the main building her duties caused her to roam throughout the building and the mortgage company in an adjoining building, smoking where-ever she went.

I visited her one morning and politely asked if she would confine her smoking to her office or the outdoor kiosk, she agreed without hesitation and I'm sure she meant it, but after a few hours she was back smoking everywhere.We recently asked all of our employees to participate in a study to see whether or not we should become a smoke free environment. A committee was made up of smokers, non-smokers and former smokers, the latter were not compromising and very vocal. The final vote was overwhelmingly in favor of not smoking.

We built an outdoor kiosk which was embarrassingly bare-bones and whenever I stopped by to visit I got an earful about how unhappy my friends were. They took great pleasure in invoking the fairness doctrine, asking how come she can smoke and we can't, or saying you should kick her out.

I was invited to an exit meeting in her smoke-filled office. She began by making some positive comments about the mortgage company and Judy Pfeffer's management, but then said, "I have a problem" which I understood to mean her problem was about to become mine.

A friend at another bank had alerted me that CRA exams were increasingly putting a lot of stress on marketing areas, so I was not completely surprised when she said we didn't seem to be making mortgage loans in the area of Blue Hill Avenue in Dorchester as required by CRA. I wanted to avoid a confrontation but her interpretation of the law was not correct.

It was my understanding that CRA required banks to meet the credit needs of all segments of the community where the bank actively received deposits. I reminded the examiner that Dorchester was part of Suffolk County and we were located in Norfolk County. For decades we were prohibited from having any branch banks beyond the county line where the home office was located. It was recently that the county line restrictions were eliminated.

My argument was it would be unwise to compete with the entrenched competition from large Boston banks like First National Bank of Boston, Shawmut Bank and Fleet.

I showed her a list of six banks with headquarters in Boston: First National Bank of Boston, Fleet, Shawmut, Bay Banks, Boston Five Cent

Savings and UST. The six banks had over 500 branches in Suffolk County. Fourteen were in Dorchester and five of the fourteen were on Blue Hill Avenue. The six banks had over $100 billion in assets. We had $1.5 billion. It seemed obvious that she had no evidence that we received any measurable deposits from the area.

I also noted that our mortgage company closed approximately $100 million in mortgage loans every year and we had not received any complaints from bank regulators, the attorney general, prospective borrowers or community action groups.

She listened politely but did not give me any indication of what rating she would recommend. I was concerned that she was on a mission with a predetermined conclusion.

The final report was the top rating. I didn't deserve any credit for the result except for letting the examiner smoke. Judy Pfeffer and her team ran the mortgage company and Graham Waiting, our chief financial officer deserved all the credit for running a great company.

My concern about CRA being used to threaten banks into reducing their mortgage underwriting standards was born out of a few years later. Paul Sperry reported that "The percentage of banks receiving the top CRA rating dropped from 24.3 percent in 1995 to 17.5 percent in 2000 and 9.5 percent in 2008."[1]

GAIL CINCOTTA, THE MOTHER OF CRA

Gail Cincotta was a community organizer from the Austin section of Chicago. In the 1970s she began fighting crime and discrimination in her neighborhood. She was a very aggressive person; one time she nailed a dead rat to an alderman's door because of his non-response to the rat infestation problem.

She staged sit ins at city council meetings and the local HUD office. Cincotta threw her support for the passage of the Home Mortgage Disclosure Act (HMDA) which drew the attention of Senator William Proxmire who invited her to testify several times at hearings.

Following the passage of HMDA, Proxmire took up the cause of passing the Community Reinvestment Act. He asked Cincotta and other civil rights leaders to draft the bill. Cincotta became known for her rallying cry, "We want it .They've got it. Let's Go Get It." She eventually was recognized as the "mother of CRA."

Proxmire was an effective legislator in spite of the fact that he was often at odds with members of his own party. He served as Chairman of the Banking, Housing and Urban Affairs Committee and he was a ranking member on the Appropriations Committee. Many remember him for his "Golden Fleece" awards for government waste.

He enlisted the support of Ted Kennedy and Frank Church in the Senate and Tip O'Neill, Speaker of the House, to guide the bill through. The CRA bill was attached to the Housing and Community Development Act, which included block grants that other Congressmen used for their pet projects.

The bill was debated one day in the Senate and there was no debate in the House. It became law on October 12, 1977. Although the law sounded rather bland, the housing activists welcomed it because it gave them a seat at the table.

President Bill Clinton early in his administration asked the bank regulators: Office of the Comptroller of the Currency, Federal Reserve, FDIC and Office of Thrift Supervision to review the CRA examination procedures to make examinations consistent and to reduce costs. Congressman Bill McCollum from Florida estimated CRA was costing banks about $1 billion per year.

Robert Rubin, Assistant to the President for Economic Policy, said changes were needed to more effectively deal with problems in the inner cities and depressed areas. Treasury Secretary Lloyd Benston said CRA needed to be strengthened to reduce redlining. Senator Proxmire was absolutely convinced that redlining was rampant and banks were guilty of "exporting capital," - that is taking deposits in one area and investing in another.

Redlining is not a well-known activity that I will describe in more detail in the next chapter.

Discussions continued over a period of time until hearings were held in 1995. Although there was some sentiment by the Republicans to repeal the act or substantially change it, in the end Senator Phil Gramm of Texas, and Congressman Bill McCollum of Florida, stood aside and President Clinton replaced all the existing CRA regulations by executive order.

Clinton instituted a numerical quota system to evaluate a bank's performance in lending to low income groups i.e. if a bank had 20 percent marketshare in a described area, it was obligated to make roughly 20 percent mortgage loans in the same area.

Clinton added another extremely important feature. CRA ratings were made public. Now the activists really had a seat at the table. A good CRA rating was necessary for regulatory approval to open or close branches, mergers, expansion, etc. Heidi Swartz, Assistant Professor at Rutgers University, quite accurately said, "CRA made it possible for activists to extract resources from banks and give them to poor and working-class families."[2]

A good example of how it worked was housing activists loudly protested the planned merger of J.P. Morgan and Chase Manhattan at a public hearing. Nothing moved until both banks pledged hundreds of thousands of dollars to various groups. It was a tactic repeated hundreds of times.

The quota system led banks that were short of the numbers for CRA loans to get the best rates to buy CRA loans from other mortgage lenders. In October 1997, First Union and Bear Stearns announced the first securitization of CRA mortgages.

Although the package may have included subprime mortgages, it was guaranteed by Freddie Mac. The deal was $385 million and was over subscribed. In the following ten months Bear Stearns sold $1.9 billion CRA mortgage loans backed by Freddie or Fannie.

President Clinton picked Janet Reno as his attorney general and she chose Deval Patrick to head the Civil Rights Division in the U.S. Department of Justice. Patrick was previously an attorney with the NAACP and he saw racism and discrimination as part of everyday life.

Patrick went on to be elected governor of Massachusetts in 2006 and over-saw the implementation of Mitt Romney's Health Care Reform law.

Reno and Patrick hired eighteen additional lawyers in the Civil Rights Division. They joined Roberta Achtenberg whom Clinton appointed assistant secretary of HUD in pursuing CRA goals.

Bill Clinton, when he was governor of Arkansas, became acquainted with Henry Cisneros who was the very popular and successful mayor of San Antonio, Texas. After Clinton was elected President he appointed Cisneros Secretary of HUD. It seemed certain to be a stepping stone for higher federal office for Cisneros.

Cisneros had been Secretary for about two years when he received a call from Mario Cuomo, then governor of New York. Governor Cuomo recommended his son Andrew as Cisneros's top aide at HUD. Andrew Cuomo was very well-connected because of his father and he was a partner in Blutrich, Falcone and Miller, a prominent law firm, especially in Democratic circles. He also was married to Robert Kennedy's daughter, Kerry, at the time.

Cuomo had created a nonprofit organization called Housing Enterprise for the Less Privileged, that built homeless shelters in New York City and the suburbs. He received praise from Mayor Dinkins and even from some Republicans.

In 1995 Cisneros began using the GSE Act of 1992 to set targets for low income loans for Fannie and Freddie. The new goals for both GSE's was 42 per cent of all their mortgage guarantees had to go for what the government defined as low-to-moderate- income borrowers.

The formal name of the GSE Act was The Federal Enterprises Financial Safety and Soundness Act of 1992. It's important because it was the first time in our history the Secretary of HUD was given authority to set housing goals and monitor compliance at Fannie and Freddie. I have written in more detail about the Act in Chapter 30.

Both Cisneros and Cuomo used the GSE Act, the Fair Housing Act, CRA and the flawed Boston Fed Mortgage Study to set mandated goals for Fannie and Freddie.

Cisneros' promising career in government came to an abrupt end in 1997 when he resigned his position due to personal problems. Andrew Cuomo quickly took over as secretary of HUD. Cuomo brought in William Apgar, a well known housing activist, as Assistant Secretary for Policy Research and Development. Apgar currently is serving as a top aide to Shaun Donovan, HUD Secretary.

It was William Apgar who initiated the decision to allow Fannie and Freddie to count subprime mortgage securities as credit for mandated goals. President Clinton issued an executive order authorizing Fannie and Freddie to buy subprime mortgage-backed securities. It was a terrible decision.

Apgar also was the person who demanded that Fannie Freddie adopt less strict requirements for credit worthiness and down payments, an equally bad decision.

Cuomo ramped up the affordable housing goals for Fannie and Freddie to 50 per cent. For every prime mortgage they financed they had to finance a nonprime mortgage. The GSE's were well on the way to failure.

Fannie and Freddie responded by buying subprime loans and securities in staggering amounts.

Their subprime loans double between 2002 and 2003 to $81 billion and doubled again in 2004 to $176 billion. In the next two years the volume was up to $279 billion in subprime loans.

Cuomo boasted about an early discrimination suit in his settlement with AccuBank Mortgage for $2.1 billion (now National City Mortgage). It was a huge settlement in 1998 and Cuomo deserved a victory lap. AccuBank may have been an unscrupulous lender but what Cuomo said after indicates he had no trouble forcing any lender to make high risk loans subject to default.

Cuomo said, "The institution would take a greater risk on these mortgages... yes, give families mortgages which they would not have been given otherwise... yes, they would not have qualified for this affirmative action on the part of the bank... yes, lending that amount $2.1 billion in mortgages will be higher risk and I'm sure there will be a higher default rates on those mortgages than the rest of the portfolio."[3]

In 1993, Roberta Achtenberg was elected as Assistant Secretary for Fair Housing and Equal Opportunity at the Department of Housing and Urban Development of (HUD). She was a former San Francisco Supervisor who is known for championing many progressive causes.

Although she has downplayed her role after the housing collapse, she was a key player in implementing the Clinton administration's agenda to increase home ownership among the disadvantaged, particularly among African-Americans and Hispanics. Achtenberg was the person responsible for monitoring Fannie's and Freddie's performance in meeting HUD goals.

She said, "standing in the way of her mission were the conservative lending policies of banks, which required such inconvenient and old-fashioned things as cash deposits and regular repayments, things the poor and minorities often could not provide."[4]

She opened 10 enforcement centers around the country with a special unit to investigate complaints, not only were complaints investigated they were solicited.

Ellen Seidman had a textbook career in Washington politics. Actually I shouldn't use the past tense, she currently is advisor to President Obama on housing policy.

Ms. Seidman served as Special Assistant for Economic Policy in the Clinton Administration 1993-1997. She was then appointed to be the Director of the Office of Thrift Supervision at the same time she was a director of the FDIC from 1997-2001. Ms. Seidman then served as Senior Counsel to Financial Services Committee of the Democrat House members

2002. At various times she held senior positions at Treasury, US Department of Transportation and Fannie Mae.

In 2009 she wrote, "the Clinton administration made CRA a priority. A major stimulus to this effect was the 1994 Riegle–Neal Interstate Banking and Branching Act which permitted, through mergers and acquisitions the nations banks we have today, that brought CRA's primary enforcement mechanisms, considerations of a bank's record of serving the community."[5]

Ms. Seidman noted in an article in Mortgage Banking that the Clinton Administration had caused the loosening of lending standards. "Financial institutions have responded by revising their underwriting practices, making lending standards more flexible. Smaller down payment requirements, more liberal rules on contributions to closing costs and reductions in cash reserve requirements have help to lower the wealth hurdle "to have home ownership."[6]

In spite of what she wrote, Seidman claimed in her article that CRA shouldn't be the scapegoat for the housing meltdown as she said in her title, "Don't Blame The Community Reinvestment Act."

It's standard practice for those who were intimately involved in President Bill Clinton's housing policies to refuse to accept any responsibility. They blame President George Bush and deregulation. Actually there was no major financial deregulation during the Bush presidency. Two major laws were passed during the Clinton administration.

The Riegle-Neal Interstate Banking and Branching Efficiency Act, 1994, and GBL 1999, which repealed the Glass-Steagall Act. Both laws made sweeping deregulation changes and both had specific provisions pertaining to CRA.

Riegle-Neal allowed banks to merge and open branches across state lines, however, the appropriate regulatory authority for approval was required to consider the banks CRA rating. GBL worked the same way. In 1989, the Federal Reserve denied a proposed merger by Continental Illinois because of an unsatisfactory CRA rating. Continental, at one time was one of the ten largest banks in the country later failed.

Janet Reno warned bankers when she took office, "Do not wait for the Justice Department to come knocking!" There are basically two reasons to agree to a settlement with the government rather than go to court: one, if you are guilty; and two, much more likely the cost of the defense is enormous and lengthy and it's punishing for the people representing the company.

I would like to comment on several settlements that I was familiar with in the early 1990s. Shawmut National Corporation had an agreement to acquire the New Dartmouth Bank. However, the Federal Reserve board refused to approve the merger because Shawmut 's record on racial fairness was not acceptable, in spite of the fact there was no record of any complaints by minorities or anyone.

The Fed referred the case to DOJ and Shawmut's Mortgage subsidiary agreed to settle out of court and pay at least $960,000 according to the Washington Times.

The Provident Institution in the Town of Boston was denied applications to open new branches until the bank agreed to increase lending in underserved areas. Provident, a grand old bank in the "town of Boston" gave up and merged with Shawmut in 1992.

New England Merchants which had been a leading bank was struggling to survive and was seeking a merger with BayBanks. Massachusetts Urban Reinvestment Advisory Group. MURAG, held up the merger until Merchants agreed to set aside 25 percent of its mortgage funds for low income minority applicants before the government allowed the merger.

A really unbelievable story is about the East Bridgewater Savings Bank in Plymouth County, Massachusetts. East Bridgewater has a population of about 3000 residents. In addition to the main office, the bank had an office in Hanson, population 2200, and an office in Pembroke, population 2000.

The bank had assets of $70 million and equity of $4.6 million. Joe Petricelli was President. He had an assistant vice president and one loan officer, several other officers and two branch managers.

In all previous CRA examinations East Bridgewater Savings had received top ratings. The bank had no foreclosures or delinquent loans, but in the recent FDIC exam it was given a "Needs to Improve" rating. It was a serious downgrade.

It was a grossly unfair and shameful decision by the FDIC. Shortly after East Bridgewater merged with Bridgewater Savings. If you were the president or trustee of a small savings bank with less than five million in capital, you would not want your bank to make many high risk mortgage loans in spite of what the FDIC required.

Paul Hancock, a Justice Department attorney who headed the Fair Lending Program said, "small banks shouldn't feel they have a safe harbor, we're not eliminating anybody from the mix here"[7]

A brief paragraph from Peter Schweitzer's book, Architects of Ruin, is illustrative of what was happening across the country. "Needless to say, banks felt the pressure even more and began giving in to the most extreme demands of the activists. In 1995, Wells Fargo agreed to a $45 billion arrangement with the California Reinvestment Committee. Washington Mutual agreed 220 billion agreement with activists in Washington state and California. In Ohio, Star Bank signed a $5 billion agreement with the Coalition on Homelessness to make loans in targeted areas."[8]

The Federal Financial Institutions Examination Council reported that during the Clinton years, CRA examinations about doubled to an average of 4750 a year. The Clinton Foundation reported that through 2000, over 90 percent of all bank loans mandated under CRA were made during eight years of the Clinton administration, 800 billion, 1993 - 2000 versus 30 billion 1977 - 1993.[9]

Washington Mutual later failed in one of the largest bank failures in US history.

I agree that not all CRA loans were bad, but this had all the earmarks of government credit allocation, under HUD mandates for Fannie and Freddie for every prime loan they purchased they had to purchase a subprime loan.

From February 1989 through 1995 HUD processed 2356 fair lending complaints; of those 2356 complaints 896 or 38 percent were settled. Another 720 cases or 31 percent where dismissed and found without merit. And 23 cases or 1 percent of the total cases were found guilty. HUD referred 9 of the 23 cases to DOJ.

Sheila Bair, a Republican from Kansas, was appointed Chairman of the FDIC by George W. Bush and reappointed by Barack Obama. When the financial crisis hit and TARP was being debated by Henry Paulson, Ben Bernanke, Tim Geithner and Bair she was treated with respect, but the FDIC was never on the same level as the Treasury, the Fed or even the Comptroller of the Currency, (the regulator of national banks.)

Chairman Bair (she used the title chairman) did an admirable job of making her voice heard in meetings. However, the charge that she often was more concerned about her reputation and her agency then the best solution for the country has some merit.

Bair's unequivocal defense of the Community Reinvestment Act overlooks how CRA was a major contributor in the failure of a number FDIC insured banks. Some were giants like Washington Mutual.

Bair spoke to the Consumer Federation of America on December 5, 2008 and said, "I want to give you my verdict on CRA: Not guilty." "Let me ask you, where in the CRA does it say to make loans to people who can't afford to repay? Nowhere."

Oh really? It was an absurd rhetorical question and the answer and was misleading. It's interesting to note that such an important issue was not listed in the index of her book under CRA or FDIC.

In mid-summer 2008, IndyMac Bank,which was founded by Angelo Mozillo and his partner at Countrywide and later spun-off was seized by the FDIC on July 11. It was the second largest bank failure after Continental in US history. IndyMac specialized in below prime rate mortgages and was a huge hit to the FDIC insurance fund of $10.7 billion.

"Bair urged President Bush to intervene with mortgage lenders to voluntarily modify loan terms, the shortfalls which would be significant were to be made up by the government not FDIC."[10]

Henry Paulson opposed the idea of government setting a precedent and voiding legal contracts. There also was concern that once such a program was started many current borrowers would stop paying and seek a government bailout.

Bair's problems were about to explode. The deluge of bank failures were as follows:

Number of Failures		Asset Size (Billions)
2008	25	373
2009	140	171
2010	157	97
	322	641

In spite of FDIC insurance there were bank runs for the first time in over 70 years

Bair presided over a tumultuous time in our financial history and she deserves much credit for her leadership. However, she devoted almost 50 pages in her book to Washington Mutual called (WaMu) but did not mention CRA even once as a significant factor as the cause of the bank's failure.

Bair wrote, "Where had WaMu gone wrong? It probably began in 2005 when it shifted its mortgage business away from fixed rate loans to subprime loans and Option ARMs with Countrywide to ramp up volume... Wa Mu had originated a significant number of "stated income" or "low dock" loans that allowed borrowers to simply write in their income on loan applications without independent verification."

"About 90 percent of WaMu home equity loans, 73 percent of its Option ARMs and half of it subprime loans were low-dock mortgages."[11]

Bair mentions the problem began in 2005, however, in 2003 the bank received the CRA Impact Award for the Community Access Program for Low Income People.

Melissa Martinez, WaMu's Chief Compliance and Risk Officer wrote an internal memo to senior management and risk personnel as follows: "risk management functions were being adapted to a "culture change" and that in the future the risk department would play a "customer service" role and avoid imposing a "burden" on "loan officers."[12]

The following story emphasizes how out-of-control things were at Wa Mu and how important CRA was. It was reported by Gretchen Morgensen and Joshua Rosner in their book "Reckless Endangerment" page 248.

Keith Johnson was an executive at WaMu in charge of a unit that specialized in small multi-family properties. It was one of the nation's largest originators of highly desirable CRA loans so Fannie and Freddie regularly courted Johnson to purchase these loans.

Johnson received a surprise call one day when he was on vacation with his family, from an executive at Freddie. The executive asked him to sell Freddie $6 billion in small multi-family loans to meet goals. It was a sham transaction. The Freddie executive said he would sell the same package back to WaMu at the same price.

After brief discussions on how WaMu would be paid, the Freddy executive agreed to pay a $100 million fee. By making the loans, WaMu had already received credits toward its obligations under CRA. Freddie could account for them as a purchase to meet its housing goals, although it really was a loan.

Regulators would later find that Fannie and Freddie, desperate to meet benchmarks, would engage in many of these dubious trades with WaMu, Citibank, and Bank of America over the years.

If you hope and believe our officials in Washington have learned from the housing collapse, you may find it discouraging to hear some of the comments that have been made in recent years.

In March, 2009, President Obama appointed Thomas Perez to head the Civil Rights Division at the Department of Justice. In the 1990s, he served as a federal prosecutor at the Department of Justice and then was promoted by Attorney General Janet Reno to deputy division chief.

Reno and Perez used "disparate impact" to determine if private housing projects violated the racial provisions of the Fair Housing Act. Disparate impact uses statistical analysis to prove discrimination and does not require discriminatory intent to prove guilt.

Perez gave a speech at the Brookings Institution in Washington, D.C. on June 23, 2010. He said, "We will require lenders to invest in the communities that they have harmed."

Mary Kissel, a member of the Wall Street Journal editorial board, wrote on August 31, 2011, that Mr. Perez testified at a congressional hearing in April, 2010 as follows: "The foreclosure crisis has touched virtually every community in this country, but it disproportionately touches communities of color, in particular African-Americans and Latinos: cross burnings are the most overt form of discrimination and bigotry."

Justice Department lawyers are supposed to interpret and enforce the laws with absolute neutrality. Equating bankers with members of the Ku Klux Klan is more than unfortunate

Mr. Perez was recently confirmed as head of the United States Department of Labor.

Chapter 15

Redlining

The term "redlining" is not well known by the general public, but it frequently was used by members of the Clinton administration when they wanted to accuse lenders of discrimination by drawing lines around neighborhoods where they would not make mortgage loans.

In the closing days of the Hoover administration the president, with the support of a Democratic Congress established the Federal Home Loan Bank system. It was designed along the lines of the Federal Reserve System and was put in place for the thrift industry to help stimulate housing recovery.

President Roosevelt established the Home Owners Loan Corporation (HOLC) in1933 and the Federal Housing Administration (FHA) the following year as major parts of his New Deal legislation.

The Home Loan Bank Board directed HOLC to refinance non-farm home mortgage loans that were in default. In a brief period of a couple of years HOLC had purchased more than 1 million loans from S&Ls and private lenders. At the high point HOLC owned more than one out of five mortgages in the US.

The HOLC program was closed down in 1935 and finally liquidated in 1951, unlike most bailouts a small profit was returned to the Treasury.

Here is the surprising part that very few know about. The Home Loan Board instructed HOLC to review 239 cities in the United States and create residential security maps to indicate the degree of risk for real estate investments (loan guarantees) in each of the cities. FHA used the maps to assess which location FHA would provide loan guarantees.

The maps were shaded blue for type A, desirable; B desirable but not as good as A and type C yellow declining and type D in red the risk category. Pictures of the old maps clearly show large areas of cities where the Federal Government would not insure mortgage loans.

Home Owners Loan Corporation generally is cited as the originator of mortgage redlining. Some of the maps that still exist contain comments that indicate sector bias and racial bias.

Eventually the federal government discontinued the practice of redlining. Unfortunately some banks and insurance companies continued the practice, but most abandoned such a crude and unwise practice years ago.

The Fair Housing Act of 1968, prohibits discrimination concerning the sale, rental and financing of houses based on race, religion and national origin.

Later, gender and disabled families with children were added to the law. Redlining with all its evil intent essentially has disappeared from the marketplace.

Chapter 16

John Kerry

I met Senator John Kerry a number of times when I was at South Shore Bank in Quincy, he was always pleasant and affable to meet with, although I'm not sure he really wanted to hear any of my opinions. The last time I met with him I was president of South Shore Chamber of Commerce and we had a small informal luncheon at the chamber.

The chamber was sometimes at odds with our elected officials but we had over 2000 members so most of the politicians welcomed the opportunity to visit and speak at various events.

During lunch I was sitting next to the Senator and on his other side was a local businessman whom I knew. We were friendly, but he was often critical of bankers in general. I heard him give Kerry some of his opinions.

After lunch Kerry made some kind remarks and then turned to me and asked if I would make a pure character loan, basically a loan based on a handshake? Before I could answer one of my directors, a very successful developer and major contributor to Democrats, said, "Well Senator, that would be a problem."

Kerry asked why, and my director went on to explain that the federal bank examiners had become very diligent, demanding documentation that any loan would be paid as agreed, which meant a record of performance and sufficient assets. Failure to satisfy the examiners could result in increased loan-loss reserves or write-downs, all of which effected earnings.

Kerry seemed surprised at federal examination procedures in spite of his long service in the Senate. After the meeting a few of us were having coffee with Kerry and he said to me, "okay, tell me a story about a character loan that would be difficult today."

I told him about a loan made by my predecessor Jack Brayton, in Fall River a number of years ago. It was about a wealthy retired textile manufacturer. He told me he went to see Brayton with his dream, but he did not have a lot of personal experience and even less in assets.

Brayton listened and asked a few questions but didn't show much enthusiasm. He said come back next week. When my friend returned, Brayton didn't waste any time in saying it's not going to work. My friend said he almost lost it, but held back.

Brayton carefully explained he liked the proposal, but the cash flow predictions were too optimistic and would become negative in six months. Brayton then said, " I really believe you are going to be successful and I am going to lend you more money than you have asked for." That was a character loan that would be difficult today.

All of that said based on my many years in the business, character is still the most important part of any loan agreement. JP Morgan said it 100 years ago when he testified before the so called Pujo committee and had the following exchange with Samuel Untermeyer, the Senate Council:

Untermyer: Is not commercial credit based primarily upon money or property?

Morgan: No, sir, the first is character!

Untermyer: Before money or property?

Morgan: Before money or anything else.[1]

PART II

The History of Banking

Chapter 17

In The Beginning

We began as a nation of farmers and the early settlers were reluctant to put much trust and confidence in a government located in big cities in New York, Philadelphia and Boston. The two early attempts to charter a United States Bank did not last very long and it would be almost 100 years before the Federal Reserve System was voted into law in 1913.

Alexander Hamilton, Secretary of the Treasury, was the leading proponent of a national bank. Thomas Jefferson was Secretary of State; James Madison, a member of Congress and Edmund Randolph, Attorney General, were aggressive in opposition.

Hamilton proposed legislation in 1790 to establish the Bank of United States. It was to be capitalized with the enormous sum at the time of $10 million. After much debate Hamilton prevailed and the charter was granted the following year.

In the early days bank charters were often granted for a period of years. When the US Bank charter came up for renewal in 1811 the opponents found an emotional issue to block the renewal. There were 25,000 shares outstanding but 18,000 of the shares were owned by foreigners. Although only U.S. citizens could vote, the foreigners did receive dividends.

The charter renewal was defeated by one vote in the House and Vice President George Clinton broke the tie in the senate and voted no. Close, but no central bank for young America.

Chapter 18

The National Bank Act

The Civil War placed a heavy burden on the Treasury to raise funds for the conduct of the war. Even today we sometimes hear our present-day currency referred to as greenbacks. In 1862 Congress authorized the treasury to issue $150 million in government bills printed in green ink and declared the notes legal tender.

It was billed as a one-time emergency measure, but our government doesn't always do what it says. Before the war ended $432 million in greenbacks were in circulation.

Although Salmon P. Chase, when he was secretary of the treasury, supported and implemented the emergency measure, eight years later as Chief Justice of the Supreme Court he found the measure unconstitutional.

The greenback plan was followed by the National Bank Act. The Act established a new system for chartering national banks, however the Federal Reserve System was still fifty years down the road.

It's hard to believe how a new system of creating money came out of the Act, but if we think about it it's not very different from how the Fed does it today.

The newly created national banks purchased government bonds and then loaned the bonds back to the government and in exchange the banks received government bills with the bank's name on the bills.

The cost to the banks was zero but technically the banks still owned the bonds so they collected interest from the government. They also had an equal amount of bills they could lend at interest.

It's not surprising the national banks found the deal very popular and the government had found a very creative way to convert government debt into money.

Although the national banks found the relationship with the government profitable, few state banks volunteered to join the national system. A favorite way our government uses to encourage behavior is through taxes. A 10 percent tax was levied on notes issued by state banks. State Banks were literally taxed into allegiance with the government.

There were so few state banks left after a while that statistics were not even kept for years. A few that were left converted to deposit banking (checking accounts) which proved so convenient and popular all banks eventually adopted deposit banking.

Chapter 19

Free Banking 1832-1863

If we were not going to have a central bank or any federal oversight of banking, the idea was why not have as many banks as possible. We began a period of free banking, sometimes called wildcat banking, from 1832 to 1863.

State legislatures began granting charters with almost no controls. Every community had a bank or banks and larger areas often had dozens. It was not unusual to have several banks in the same building, some were on the upper floors of city buildings.

Massachusetts had a generally good record of few bank failures, but there was a bank that issued $500,000 of its banknotes backed by only $86.48 in gold coins.

There were widespread abuses around the country. Two requirements to get a charter were really bizarre. One was the organizers could commit to buying a certain amount for the capital, but only pay for a fractional amount of that total; the other was the organizers could borrow as much as the full amount for their shares from the bank being organized.

It didn't take long for the lax chartering and little or no supervision to result in hundreds of failures. In the pre-FDIC era many depositors were wiped out. One bank failure often led to a run on other banks, causing more failures.

The hardship resulting from widespread failures demonstrated the need for more careful chartering, including full paid-in capital and state regulation and supervision.

The stricter requirements also brought a sense that the federal government or the state in granting a charter meant the recipient would have a protected franchise, free from unregulated competition and as such there was a responsibility to give something back to the community.

There also was an imbedded idea that the local community should be protected, especially thrift banks, and we should steadfastly resist a concentration in banking by giant banks.

Chapter 20

The Second Bank Of The United State

The War of 1812 is often described as one of the most senseless wars in history. Our history books say the primary cause was the British Navy capturing two American sailors and forcing them to join in the fight against France in the Napoleonic War.

England quickly abandoned their policy, but the war was soon underway. The two seamen from New England were released. The New England states generally were against the war. The Western and Southern states generally supported the war.

Whatever lay beyond the reason or several reasons for the war, we will never know, but it is certain the cost of the war caused an explosion in the money supply and in our national debt.

In 1816 the Second Bank of United States was charted by Congress for a period of 20 years.

Its purpose was to restore the stability of the money supply and available credit.

Nicholas Biddle, a name some of us remember from long-ago history lessons, became the director and driving force of the Second Bank. Biddle was born into a wealthy Philadelphia family. In his very early years he was described as brilliant and in fact he graduated from the University of Pennsylvania at the age of thirteen.

He was also called arrogant, ruthless, and driven. The banks headquarters in Philadelphia was worthy of a Washington, DC government building. It was as imposing as a Greek temple. It had branches across state lines, something generally not permitted for banks during much of our history.

The Second Bank had an exclusive franchise to maintain all federal deposits at no interest, an enormously profitable monopoly. The real and perceived privilege and special federal relationship over time made Biddle and his bank a very powerful business enterprise and political force.

Biddle rewarded his friends and supporters generously and believed he was beyond the reach of Federal interference or control.

President Jackson, a populist, ranted against privilege and harbored an extreme dislike for Biddle. It appeared he would run for reelection on the anti-bank, anti privilege platform.

Biddle decided in 1832 to seek a renewal charter for the bank four years before it's charter was due to expire. He wanted to preempt the president before he gained more power and confidently he believed he would prevail.

Both sides indulged in an acrimonious and very personal debate. Biddle said, "This worthy President thinks because he has scalped Indians and imprisoned a judge, he is to have his way with the bank. He is mistaken."

Biddle believed he had won when the renewal charter passed both houses of Congress. President Jackson defiantly vetoed the bill and went public with his reasons:

1. The Bank was unconstitutional
2. It was a monopoly
3. Foreign investment could exert some influence and control.

Jackson's veto held and he quickly moved to withdraw all government funds.

End of story...not quite!

The bank still had four years left on its original charter and Biddle was not without weapons to retaliate. He severely contracted the money supply and available credit. He hoped to create a panic which would be blamed on the president and in fact he did create a downturn and recession.

The Senate voted 26-22 to censure the president, the first president to ever be censored by the United States Senate. Jackson referred to the senators as a den of vipers.

After Biddle's bank lost its federal charter it was granted a charter by the state of Pennsylvania. However, having lost it special relationship with the Federal Government it failed in 1841.

Congress passed a vote to investigate whether Biddle's bank had deliberately caused the crisis. When federal investigators arrived at his bank he brazenly refused them entry.

In time he was accused of improperly using bank funds to speculate in cotton futures. He was arrested on fraud charges but was found not guilty on criminal charges. He died while the civil case was pending.

Chapter 21

The Federal Reserve

It's a very strange story about how the Federal Reserve became what some people call the Fourth Branch of Government. It didn't originate in the halls of Congress or in the White House; it began at J.P. Morgan's private club at Jekyll Island, Georgia.

In early 1907 the stock market took a steep dive and there was concern it would turn into a crash. Jacob Schiff with Kuhn Loeb, Henry Clay Frick, U.S. Steel, Edward Harriman, Southern Pacific Railroad and William Rockefeller held a meeting to construct a plan to save the economy. They believed a $25 million fund might be needed.

They wanted to enlist J.P. Morgan as a member of their group, however his initial reaction was not to join. Perhaps the expectation that Morgan would join led to a brief market rally but by October the market was in free-fall in what became known as the crash of 1907.

Morgan was 70 years old and semi retired and was attending an Episcopal convention as a delegate in Richmond, Virginia, when he received an urgent call for help. Morgan returned to New York and became a one-man central bank. President Teddy Roosevelt, a progressive who spoke out about "the money trust" had such a high regard for Morgan he had his secretary of the treasury, George Cortelyou make $25 million in U.S. Treasuries available for Morgan's rescue efforts.

Morgan and his partners helped the City of New York roll over $30 million in bonds. They advanced $25 million to keep the stock exchange open and when more was needed they advanced another $13 million.

Although it's taken for granted today that large commercial banks have trust divisions, back then bankers were prohibited from directly engaging in the trust business, however the prohibition did not prevent banks from owning separate trust companies. Morgan via voting trusts controlled Bankers Trust and Guarantee Trust, both very large organizations.

A number of the independent trust companies with minimum capital, however, engaged in highly speculative trading with customers funds.

The Knickerbocker Trust Company is a sad example that is often pictured in old newspaper clippings and stories. The pictures show long lines of customers crowding the sidewalks to withdraw their funds at the bank on 34th Street and Fifth Avenue.

Charles Barney, the President of Knickerbocker, called Morgan for help, but after Morgan's examiners reported on gross mismanagement, Morgan, also a shareholder, declined to help. Barney committed suicide and the failure of his bank led to a run on other banks, including a run on the Trust Company of America where Morgan also was a shareholder. Morgan stepped in to save the bank and several others.

In spite of the extraordinary performance of J.P. Morgan we reached a turning point in our history. There was a public outcry for banking reform and federal regulation. In 1908 Congress passed the Aldrich-Vreeland Act which created the National Monetary Commission. It's an unbelievable story of how the Federal Reserve came into being. The Act was named after Nelson Aldrich, a Republican senator from Rhode Island and Edward Vreeland, a former banker from Buffalo.

Aldrich spent two years studying central banking in England and Europe at the taxpayers' expense. He compiled his information in 30 volumes, none of which he shared with his congressional colleagues.

The commission included nine senators and nine representatives with Aldrich as chairman and Vreeland vice chairman. The extraordinary fact is that Vreeland and the congressional members of the commission never participated in any discussions, deliberations nor were any of them consulted for their opinions. It's also strange there is little record of complaints from the members about being left out of such important legislation.

In December 2013, there were many articles on the 100th anniversary of the Fed. Two of the best books currently available on the subject are "The Creature from Jekyll Island" by G. Edward Griffin and "Secrets of the Temple" by William Grieder.

Griffin wrote at length about the extreme secrecy of the meeting at Jekyll Island. There is some uncertainty about the attendees at the meeting, but Griffin lists the following six participants.

- Senator Nelson Aldrich, Republican from Rhode Island
- Henry Davison, Senior Vice President, J.P. Morgan
- Charles Norton, President, First National Bank (New York)
- Frank Vanderlip, President, National City Bank (New York)
- Benjamin Strong, Bankers Trust Company (owned by J.P. Morgan)
- Paul Warburg, Partner, Kuhn Loeb

It's obvious that the number of New York bankers and influence of Morgan opened the gates for criticism by the opponents of the Aldrich Plan.

Aldrich wanted to be remembered as the author of the Federal Reserve Act, however he became ill during the deliberations. Edward Griffin wrote in his book that it was Paul Warburg who was the major author. Griffin quoted Prof. Edwin Seligman to back up his claim as follows, "in it's fundamental features the Federal Reserve Act is the work of Mr. Warburg more than any other." Paul Warburg had been in the country only six years when he was appointed to the new Federal Reserve Board of Governors. When World War I broke out he resigned because of his concern that his relationship with I. G. Farben was a conflict.[1]

In spite of the attempt to conceal who the participants were at Jekyll Island and what recommendations they would make, information began to leak out. Senator Lafollette denounced the money trust saying, "They selected people who had the power to disperse or withhold prosperity."

Congressman Charles Lindbergh said, "the Aldrich Plan is the Wall Street Plan. It means another panic if necessary to intimidate the people."

Senator Aldrich, in addition to being a sponsor of a new central bank, was also one of the proponents of the federal income tax. The income tax that President Lincoln imposed during the war was declared unconstitutional in 1895.

In the tumult of the period the 16th Amendment was passed in 1913 to establish a federal income tax.

The Democrats could took control of the house in 1910 and the Senate in 1912 and Senator Aldrich was defeated for reelection. Woodrow Wilson was elected president.

President William Howard Taft was running for reelection and in the early polls he had a good lead over Woodrow Wilson. Taft had publicly stated he was opposed to a central bank and would veto any bill to establish one.

Several of the prominent New York bankers that were supporting the creation of a central bank, including Jacob Schiff, the director of Kuhn Loeb, backed Teddy Roosevelt of the Progressive Party. J.P. Morgan and Company provided the financial backing for Roosevelt's campaign. The Republican vote was split and Wilson won the presidency with 42 per cent of the popular vote.

Carter Glass became chairman of the House banking committee. He acknowledged he was not expert in banking or finance, however he was given the task of rewriting the Aldrich Plan. He succinctly and reasonably raised the following questions:

There was little or no government control.

There was way too much concentration of power given to New York banks.

The cost to the taxpayers was underestimated.

The Federal Reserve Act was passed on December 23, 1913. Although much of Aldrich's Plan was scrapped, the Democrats agreed to several important concessions.

The Act established a board of governors appointed by the president, subject to senate confirmation. A major concession allowed voluntary membership for state banks, however national banks were required to belong.

The 12 regional Federal Reserve Banks were Aldrich's idea to deflect some of the criticism of a too powerful central bank. The New York Fed has always been first among equals and the regional banks have steadily lost power over the years.

MARRINER STODDARD ECCLES

The story of Marriner Stoddard Eccles is an interesting and not well known American story. Mariner Eccles' father had emigrated from Scotland in his early teens. He never learned to read or write, but he had a knack for business and in time he owned a number of companies, a railroad and a bank. He was a Mormon and had two wives and twenty-one children. He believed in hard work, thrift and no debt.

Mariner was 22-years-old when his father died and he took over his father's business empire and became the head of both families. He inherited his father's business acumen.

Eccles was head of his bank in Ogden, Utah when the Depression caused the failure of many banks across the country. His bank narrowly survived and he was invited to testify before a senate committee.

During his senate testimony in 1933 he urged the government to spend public funds for unemployment relief, public works, agriculture, and farm mortgage assistance.

He proposed federal insurance of bank deposits - something FDR initially rejected - the redistribution of income, a strong central bank, a minimum wage and the regulation of the stock market. It seems he outlined most of the "New Deal" before the president.

President Roosevelt appointed him to the Federal Reserve Board in 1934 and he set out to reorganize and modernize the institution. He recommended removing the Secretary of the Treasury and Comptroller of the Currency, both appointees of the president, from the board. In spite of his close relationship with the president the change removed significant influence of the president over the Fed. Another important change he instituted was the regional Fed bank's role in setting interest rates. It was transferred to the Federal Open Market Committee, FOMAC.

The original Act was significantly amended during President Roosevelt's administration and like most laws there have been other amendments. The current law is 88 pages long and it is very explicit and detailed regarding the Fed's powers. We could assume if something is not described in the law then the board could not do it, however there is an extremely important provision in section 13, Powers of the Federal Reserve Board called, "Board Action in Necessary and Exigent Circumstances. (Page 35)

It grants the Federal Reserve extremely broad powers to make loans to other than Fed members, "to prevent, correct, or mitigate serious harm to the economy or stability of the financial system to the United States."

A few companies received help during the Depression but it was very modest by today's standards.

During the discussion of the bailout of AIG Ben Bernanke and Henry Paulson briefed congressional leaders regarding their plan. Later Congressman Barney Frank recalled asking Ben Bernanke "if he had $80 billion for the bailout"and Bernanke replied, "well, we have 800 billion if needed.

Frank said, "it was the first time that many of us understood the full scope of the "necessary and exigent circumstances statute."[2]

Chapter 22

The Savings Industry Disappears

Thrift banks include mutual savings banks, savings and loan associations, cooperative banks and credit unions; all are mutual organizations owned by their depositors or members.

As mutual banks without shareholders they enjoyed a philanthropic image and received special treatment from Congress and state legislators. For years they were granted a special rate advantage under that infamous Regulation Q which allowed them to pay a slightly higher rate on regular savings accounts than commercial banks.

In fact national banks where prohibited from making home mortgage loans until the passage of the McFadden Act in 1927, even then for the next 20 years they could only lend on appraised value for five-year maturities. State banks generally were allowed to make mortgage loans, but for many years they could only make non-amortizing loans.

The savings and loans pioneered a very important innovation in the early years: the amortizing mortgage. Instead of just paying interest and no principal on the loan the borrower had the opportunity to become a real homeowner.

The first mutual savings bank in the U.S. was the Provident Institution for Savings in the Town of Boston, which was incorporated in 1816. The Provident was a grand old bank for 175 years before merging with Shawmut Corporation in 1992. Shawmut has also disappeared.

Mutual savings banks were primarily in the Northeast, in 1982 there were 266 mutuals in New England and 95 in New York out of a total of 424 in the country.

Savings and loan associations were originally known as building and loans and began in 1831. The S & Ls rapidly spread throughout the country.

I would guess that students taking a class in money and banking today would assume that the highly specialized thrift banks had lobbied hard for years for expanded powers to become full-service banks, but the opposite is the case. They used their significant political clout to oppose any deregulation that would jeopardize their savings rate differential.

In the 1980s inflation and rapidly rising rates were creating great stress for thrifts; their portfolios were full of long-term mortgages paying substantially less than they were paying on deposits. Borrowing short and lending long is an age-old problem in banking. The academics came up with an inflated description calling it "term structure risk." The solution was to expand lending powers so that Thrifts "could grow out of their problems."

It was a matter of survival; the thrifts had to give up their savings rate advantage to gain authority to expand lending. The move from relatively safe home mortgage loans into higher-yielding commercial loans with much less security also brought much greater risks. Commercial real estate loans are among the highest risk category.

The Depository Institutions Deregulation and Monetary Control Act of 1980, which passed with the support of President Jimmy Carter, began the wholesale deregulation of the thrift industry.

All banks were given authority to offer interest-bearing checking accounts and consumer loans. The Merrill Lynch Money Markets Account and the NOW Account were rapidly changing customer payment options.

During the time I was in the consulting business I did some work for a large mutual fund. Although the people I worked with were very polite, there was a general impatience and perhaps disdain for the staid old world of banking.

I observed a large numbers of people who took the elevator to the sixth floor every day to obtain a prospectus or open a money market account.

Thrifts, unlike commercial banks that can raise capital by selling stock, had to rely on retained earnings.

The Federal Home Loan Bank Board began reducing restrictions on the investments its members could make and unfortunately began allowing very questionable accounting procedures to conceal mounting losses of its members. It would be easy to predict it would not end well.

In October 1982, Ferdinand St. Germain, Chairman of the House

Banking Committee who was a Democrat from Rhode Island and Jake Garn, Chairman of the Senate Banking Committee and a Republican from Vermont, proposed the Garn-St. Germain Depository Institutions Act. It passed both houses of Congress and was signed by Ronald Reagan. President Reagan said, "I think we hit a home run."

The elimination of regulations relating to commercial real estate lending was stunning. It allowed an S&L to lend up to 100 percent of the bank's capital to any one borrower. It didn't take a skilled bank examiner to figure out one such failed loan spelled the failure of the S&L.

The Home Loan Bank Board required a member bank to have a net worth equal to only 5 percent of uninsured deposits. However, if that seemed rather harsh, the S&L was given twenty-five years to reach the target.

The earlier legislation, DIDMCA, eliminated the requirement that prohibited S&Ls from obtaining more than 5 percent of total deposits from money brokers. Although it was a known problem, Garn-St. Germain deliberately did not change the rule.

The Bank Board also allowed several dubious ways of financial accounting: one of the worst was known as Memorandum R – 49. It had to do with accounting for losses on assets that were sold and was known as loss-deferred. Instead of recognizing the loss when it incurred it was written off over ten years. There were other highly questionable accounting practices that were allowed.

In 1987, Stuart Root, a prominent New York lawyer became a director of the Federal Savings and Loan Insurance Corporation, (FSLIC) and he quickly became a powerful voice in what was essentially an insolvent government insurance fund.

Root was convinced that the S&L problems could be solved given time and reasonable government help. Root previously had represented the Bowery Savings Bank and he picked Bud Gravette, a former Bowery officer, to visit the Texas S&Ls that were in trouble and to work out a plan.

Gravette suggested the problems could be solved by merging the failing S&Ls into larger ones and the cost to the insurance fund would be in the range of $10 - 12 billion. The capital infusions to attract new investors would need government guarantees of questionable assets and maybe income. It became known as the Southwest Plan and facilitated the consolidation of 220 S&Ls in 1998. Of that number 88 were in Texas; of course the problems were far from over.

Charles Keating and his Lincoln Savings and Loan is a special story. Keating's company, American Continental Corporation, acquired Lincoln S&L with the help of Michael Milken. Keating also met Ivan Boesky, the arbitrage king, through Milken; all three went to prison.

Keating wasted little time in converting Lincoln S&L from a traditional home mortgage loan company to an Arizona land developer operation. He fired most of the management at Lincoln, stopped writing mortgages and operated primarily with brokered deposits. Keating invested heavily in land deals, mortgage-backed securities and derivatives.

He exploited all the creative accounting procedures allowed and operated with little regulation. His holding company (ACC) went bankrupt in 1989 and Lincoln soon failed and was taken over by the FDIC. The cost was $3 billion, the largest S&L failure in US history.

Toby Roth, a Republican congressman from Wisconsin, said at a hearing with bank regulators on October 31, 1989, "The summation of testimony, as I see it, is basically that Keating used a federally insured S&L to operate a carefully planned looting and he had the umbrella of political protection to keep you at bay." His last sentence regarding political protection was at the heart of Keating's crimes.[1]

The Senate ethics committee found Alan Cranston, (D-Ca.), Dennis DeConcini, (D-Az.) and Donald Riegle (D-Mi.), interfered with the Federal Home Loan Bank Board investigation of the failure of Lincoln.

Cranston received a formal reprimand but remained defiant. Riegal apologized and DeConcini refused to acknowledge any wrongdoing.

John Glenn and John McCain were criticized for poor judgment. The issue came up briefly during the 2008 presidential campaign.

The problem in the thrift industry was barely mentioned during the presidential campaign between George H.W. Bush and Michael Dukakis in 1998, but after his election President Bush announced a bailout plan for the Thrift banks. The law that resulted is the Financial Institutions Reform, Recovery, and Enforcement Act, 1989, (FIRREA).

There is a troubling provision in the new law that Martin Mayer wrote about, "buried in FIRREA was a provision that denied bank and S&L examiners the whistle blower protection given almost all of the federal employees. A dismissed SNL examiner named Trish Cosgrove, a staid bespectacled young lady who looked like central castings idea of a librarian, couldn't find anyone in the House or Senate Banking Committee willing to sponsor repeal of that provision - though all other reforms will be stymied if examiners can be punished "by superiors acting at the behest of administrators who may be acting for political reasons."[2]

It was a repugnant addition to the law done anonymously by some government official, however the law did repeal many of the abuses of the previous legislation. The words Reform and Recovery in the title of the law were well off the mark. Reform and Recovery meant a $50 billion fund to finance a new federal agency, the Resolution Trust Company, RTC, to act as the receiver of failed S&Ls.

It sounded like a large fund that the tax-payers were on the hook for because the savings insurance fund (FSLIC) was broke. The number of failed S&Ls and savings banks was higher than expected, but the real problem was that the final losses on all the failed thrifts was much more than projected.

The final cost of the bailout of the thrifts was $153 billion and the inflation adjusted cost is $256 billion.

The new law did away with the Federal Home Loan Bank Board and replaced it by the Office of Thrift Supervision, OTS, which was part of the Treasury Department. FSLIC, the insurance fund was replaced by the Savings Insurance Fund as part of the FDIC.

Many thrifts converted to stock ownership and gave up their special niche as the workingman's bank. Securitization of mortgage loans made it possible for commercial banks, Wall Street banks and a new group of fierce competitors, and the private mortgage companies to write loans, collect fees and sell loans to Fannie and Freddie. Savings deposits were no longer needed to fund the business.

The thrifts have left the scene in massive numbers, however credit unions have surged in their place, largely because they are exempt from federal taxes and exempt from the Community Reinvestment Act.

Part III

An Exploration and Analysis Of The Recent Financial Crisis

Chapter 23

The Twins: Fannie And Freddie

I began writing this book more than two years ago and I believed based on my years of experience in banking and my knowledge of the housing market that the housing collapse and financial crisis was primarily caused by our national housing policies.

I did not find much support for my conclusion until much later, and in fact after reading dozens and dozens of books and countless academic reports and articles about the crisis, almost all of the authors agree there were multiple causes, but very few found Fannie and Freddie as major causes of the housing collapse. The Community Reinvestment Act (CRA) received some criticism by several but was ignored or hardly mentioned by others.

One of the most outspoken was Barry Ritholtz, a regular on CNBC and author of Bailout Nation. He wrote in 2009, only months after the crash, "CRA was irrelevant to the current crisis, Fannie Mae and Freddie Mac were mere cogs in a complex machine with many moving parts. But the primary cause of the mess? Not even close."[1]

Ritholtz wrote about his disdain for people who disagreed with him as trying to rewrite history. He and others regularly complain, how can anything like Fannie which has been on the books for 70 years be the blamed for the financial crisis.

The reality is history often is rewritten because the early reports on major events are time-sensitive and need to be produced quickly. In the longer view and perhaps with less emotion and personal bias, writers have access to new information that may modify or change earlier reports.

Almost 100 years after the Great Depression books are still being written about the causes and the government response. I suspect the same will be true of our recent financial crisis. I don't believe Fannie and Freddie were mere cogs in a complex machine. They could not have reached such massive size and dominance in the mortgage market without the extraordinary pressure from two administrations and the full support of the Congress.

President Franklin Roosevelt in the depths of the Great Depression in 1938 proposed legislation to create the Federal National Mortgage Association, now known as Fannie Mae. The legislation was in response to the flood of home foreclosures, bank failures and a frozen mortgage market.

Mortgage loans at the time where primarily made by savings and loan associations and mutual savings banks. The loans were portfolio loans retained on the bank's books until paid off. As such, underwriting standards were strict.

Monthly payments generally could not exceed 28 percent of the borrowers income, down payments were substantial and there were a number of other requirements, including verification of income, a personal interview and a formal closing.

It's surprising that in the early years Fannie actually imposed a conservative influence on the way banks approved loans.

Fannie Mae's mission was to sell bonds to the public with a government guarantee the proceeds from the sale of the bonds was used to buy mortgage loans from the banks and the payment on the loans was used to pay off the bonds.

Houses were much smaller in the 1930s and 1940s, generally under 950 feet of living space. They generally consisted of two bedrooms, one bath, one car garage and small lot. The thrifts had the bulk of their assets concentrated in local mortgage loans. It didn't take much of a decline in house prices to cause defaults and foreclosures and ultimately bank failures. Between 1930 and 1939 over one third of the S&Ls and mutuals closed. The numbers declined from 11,800 to 7,500.

In 1968 President Lyndon Johnson was informed by the Comptroller General that Fannie's budget would have to be included in the president's federal budget. Johnson was struggling with the Vietnam War and at the same time trying to advance his "war on poverty" and "Great Society" programs. Johnson proposed legislation to remove Fannie from the federal budget.

The legislation enacted by Congress made Fannie a public/private corporation with public shareholders and public and government directors. The legislation also provided a new corporation: the Federal Home Loan Mortgage Corporation, now known as Freddie Mac. Freddie began business in 1970. Its original purpose was to help the struggling savings and loan industry, however in time Freddie was given expanded powers to compete directly with Fannie.

Prior to the new legislation Fannie's guarantee of its debts, (bonds, etc.) was a full guarantee. The debts of both Fannie and Freddie became implied government guarantees.

A similar budget question regarding the two GSE's came up early in the Obama administration. Peter Orzag, CBO Director, said he intended to include Fannie and Freddie budgets in the federal budget because of the degree of control (ownership) by the government after the takeover.

Jim Nussle, the White House budget director, disagreed, declaring the government takeover was temporary. The definition of temporary may not be exact but here we are five years later and our government remains in control.

Fannie and Freddie performed their mission very well for many years, but were corrupted by greedy executives and turned into failed social experiments by the United States Government.

Chapter 24

James Johnson

To understand how Fannie Mae and Freddie Mac acquired such political influence to become the dominant players in the U.S. housing market, one has to examine the rolls of several key executives - James Johnson and Franklin Raines at Fannie Mae and Richard Syron at Freddie. History should judge them very harshly for their participation in the destruction of Fannie Mae and Freddie Mac.

James Johnson was a charming, extremely ambitious young guy from Minnesota who became the consummate insider in the Democratic Party. He was the chief executive officer of Fannie Mae from 1991 to 1999 and in that short period of time he made Fannie into one of the largest corporations in the world. He also led the way in dismantling many of the traditional standards for approving mortgage loans.

He began his career working in Eugene McCarthy's and George McGovern's presidential campaigns. He then served as Vice President Walter Mondale's executive assistant in the Jimmy Carter administration.

in 1980, after Jimmy Carter lost his bid for re-election to Ronald Reagan, James Johnson left government service and joined Richard Holbrooke. They started a consulting firm called Public Strategies. It's probably not surprising that Fannie Mae was one of the first clients.

Although he had never run a company or large organization he was picked to become Chairman and Chief Executive Officer of Fannie Mae in 1991. He established himself as the person to dramatically change the way Fannie did business and transform the market.

Shortly after joining Fannie he announced a one trillion dollar program to help ten million families become home owners. He said the program was, "a promise to do for lower income and minority groups, the elderly, new immigrants and residents of inner cities what Fannie had long done for the broad suburban middle-class."

"The idea is to bring Fannie's financial muscle to bear, creating partnerships with housing advocacy groups, community development organizations, lenders, homebuilders and real estate agents."[1]

In 1996, Johnson claimed that Fannie had helped more than two million families become home owners the previous year. Johnson said, "the first half of this decade has been a period of exciting new activity on the affordable lending front. Our customers (banks and mortgage companies) stepped up to the challenge of providing more access to mortgage credit for low and moderate income families, minorities, new immigrants and other Americans with special housing needs."[2]

Fannie Mae, under Johnson's leadership, embarked on a new activist housing mission much like ACORN and other housing activist groups. Johnson advised lenders to be more flexible when they reviewed applicants assets and income, he said, "primary income may be supplemented by income from family members who are on disability or work off the books." "Fannie Mae also encouraged lenders to give mortgages to certain nonpermanent immigrants also known as illegal immigrants."[3]

Natasha Schulman added, "it was not unusual for some immigrants to have more than one Social Security number."[4]

Fannie and Freddie's balance sheet of mortgages owned and their off-balance-sheet guarantees were skyrocketing in the period 2005 to 2007 and they were heading for $1 trillion subprime and ALt-A loans. ALt-A loans are generally described as not quite prime and not quite subprime.

Johnson was was skillful in courting and rewarding members of Congress and equally successful in blocking any legislation that would curtail Fannie's activities. The top twenty-five recipients of Fannie and Freddie campaign contributions, including PACs and individuals received more than $1.3 million dollars between 1989 and 2008.

The above numbers are from a chart in Paul Sperry's book, "The Great American Bank Robbery" page 220. Sperry's source was the Federal Election Commission on June 30, 2008 FEC, Center for Responsive Politics.

In 1993 Johnson came up with a brilliant idea to open partnership offices in various cities around the country. The offices were opened with much fanfare and media coverage. Local members of Congress and candidates of course were headlined. It was standard practice to staff the offices with relatives and friends of the elected officials.

One of the first offices to open was in Boston. Senator Kennedy who was in a tight race for reelection with Mitt Romney was the featured speaker at the opening.

When the Atlanta office was opened in 1995, Newt Gingrich, then Speaker of the House, and an advocate for limited government, said at the opening, "Fannie Mae is an excellent example of a former government institution fulfilling its mandate while functioning in the market economy." Gingrich later did consulting for Fannie.

In 1996 Senator "Kit" Bond, a Republican from Missouri, was in attendance when Johnson opened the Kansas City office. In 1999 a partnership office was opened in Utah. A former legislative aide to Sen. Robert Bennett was made head of the office and Bennett's son was an employee. Bennett was one of the largest recipients of donations from Fannie and Freddie.

I have further comments on both Sen. Bond and Sen. Bennett in the chapter about the scandals involving both Fannie and Freddie.

Johnson retired in 1999 a very wealthy man after a relatively short run at Fannie. During his tenure there was a pervasive atmosphere of secrecy regarding Johnson's compensation and other financial matters, all of which should have been disclosed to the board of directors and shareholders. Congressman Richard Baker, a Republican from Louisiana, said he intended to disclose information about executive compensation at Fannie and was immediately threatened with a personal lawsuit.

The outrageous threat became moot when the financial scandal broke that disclosed lavish pay and bonus programs and fraudulent accounting practices that depicted both GSEs as corrupt organizations.

Johnson's retirement package was off the charts. He had a post retirement contract that paid him $350,000 per year, two employees, a car and driver and an office suite in the Watergate complex. He also receives a pension of $71,000 per month ($852,000 per year) for life. He was 56 years old when he retired. He has since given up a few of the benefits.

After retiring from Fannie he joined the board of Goldman Sachs and served on the Compensation Committee that approved Henry Paulson's salary.

Barack Obama asked Johnson to participate on the committee to vet potential vice president candidates. It was widely agreed Johnson was angling to be appointed Secretary of the Treasury.

His charmed life crashed when it was learned he had received numerous mortgages for millions of dollars from "the Friends of Angelo" program at Countrywide. Johnson was quietly dropped from the Obama team.

Chapter 25

Franklin Raines

Franklin Delano Raines followed James Johnson as chief executive of Fannie Mae in 1999. It was a great American success story that unfortunately did not have a happy ending.

He graduated from Harvard College and Harvard Law School and began his political career in several positions in the Carter Administration. He left public life to join Lazard-Freres, where he stayed for eleven years and became a partner and vice-chairman.

He left Lazard in 1996 to join the Clinton Administration as Director of Management and Budget. When James Johnson retired from Fannie, Raines was elected president. He was recognized as the first African–American to run a Fortune 500 company. Unlike Johnson, who had no business background, Raines had an enviable resume.

Shortly after joining the company Fannie met the goal of providing $1 trillion in loans for underserved communities. Without hesitation he increased the goal to $2 trillion to help 18 million more families become first-time home buyers.

The same year in July 1999, "Andrew Cuomo proposed stricter requirements for Fannie and Freddie. The share of mortgages to be granted to those earning less than the median income in their area was raised from 42 to 52 percent, and the share that should go to people on very low incomes increase from 14 to 20 percent. The Chairman of Fannie Mae, Franklin D Raines, was very receptive to the new message: "We have not been a major presence in the subprime market, but you can bet that under these goals we will be."[1]

Raine's didn't hesitate in launching a huge subprime project in September.

He launched a $2 trillion "Dream Commitment" program to expand homeownership to 18 million low income earners and minorities. In 2000 Fannie bought only $1.2 billion in subprime mortgages, in 2001 the number was up to $9 billion and in 2002 the number was $15 billion. By 2004 Fannie and Freddie together purchased $175 billion in subprime loans.

Steven Holmes gave an early warning that was largely ignored. Holmes said, "In moving even tentatively into this new area of lending Fannie Mae is taking on significantly more risk, which may not pose any difficulties during flush economic times. But the government subsidized corporations may run into trouble in an economic downturn, prompting a government rescue similar to that of the savings and loan industry in the 1980s."[2]

Holmes' warning of the possibility of an economic downturn was ignored by the best financial minds in the country. Hardly anyone predicted the dramatic decline in house prices that would lead to a housing collapse and financial crisis.

Fannie and Freddie opened up the market for renters to become house buyers, not necessarily homeowners. The GSEs also made it possible for a whole new category of players known as "flippers" to enter the market. These were not traditional homebuyers but gamblers, all of which drove up house prices, but as it always happens bubbles burst.

Chapter 26

President George W. Bush

George W. Bush was elected president in 2001 and like Bill Clinton he served for two terms. Although President Bush lacked several of the colorful and aggressive housing activists in the Clinton administration he in many ways followed the Clinton agenda on home ownership.

He picked Mel Martinez, a Cuban immigrant to succeed Andrew Cuomo as secretary of HUD. Martinez immediately increased the goals that Cuomo had set for home ownership from 50 percent to 52 percent. Martinez said he believed in universal home ownership for minorities.

Martinez left HUD in November of 2004 to return to Florida to run for the Senate. He was succeeded by Alphonso Jackson, an African-American, who also believed in increased home ownership for all Americans, especially for minorities.

The HUD budget is enormous and Jackson won high marks for implementing management controls that led to significant improvements.

In 2008, he was accused of receiving special below-market rate loans from Countrywide Financial. He denied any knowledge of special loans, but resigned his position. He went on to serve as the Distinguished University Professor and Director of the Center for Public Policy and Leadership at Hampton University, Hampton, Virginia.

President George W. Bush said in 2002, shortly after he was elected president, "We can put light where there is darkness, and hope where there's despondency in this country. And part of it is working together as a nation to encourage folks to own their own home."[1]

I assume President Bush meant his statement to be inspiring and demonstrate his compassionate conservatism. However, he did not give any specific goals until his speech at a day long conference on housing sponsored by the White House at Georgetown University in October 2002.

In his opening speech President Bush spoke about expanding home ownership for minorities. He said, "I've issued a challenge to everyone involved in the housing industry to help increase the number of minority families to be homeowners. I'm talking about bankers and your brokers and developers...22 public and private partners have signed up to help meet our national goal...Partners in the mortgage finance industry are encouraging home ownership by purchasing more loans made by banks to African-Americans, hispanics and other minorities."[2]

He occasionally made a few of his remarks in Spanish.

The following year President Bush supported the American Dream Down Payment Act which would subsidize down payments and closing costs for low income minority borrowers. He signed the legislation on December 16, 2003. In his remarks at the signing he praised Franklin Raines, CEO of Fannie, for helping to dismantle barriers to home ownership. He mentioned a Fannie Mae outreach program that helped deserving families with bad credit histories to qualify for mortgage loans. The Act provided up to $1,500 for closing costs and down payments.

"The share of home loans purchased by Fannie and Freddie with a down payment of 5 percent or less were 3.3 percent at Fannie and 1.1 percent at Freddie in 1977. This rose to 26 percent at Fannie and 19.3 percent at Freddie in 2007. The total for both companies for the same period rose from 4.4 percent to 45.3 percent."[3]

Paul Sperry wrote that "Secretary Martinez helped push a major increase in subprime loans originated by Fannie and Freddie from 2002 to 2006 from $204 billion to $591 billion. Mortgage-backed securities purchased by Fannie and Freddie went from $38 billion in 2003 to $110 billion in 2006."[4]

Secretary of the Treasury John Snow testified before the House Financial Service Committee on September 10, 2003: "There is a general recognition that the supervisory system for housing-related GSEs neither has the tools nor stature to deal effectively with the current size, complexity and importance of these two enterprises."[5]

George Bush supported the recommendation by Treasury Secretary Snow to transfer the regulatory and supervisory authority of both Fannie and Freddie to a new agency in the Treasury Department.

Alan Greenspan joined Secretary Snow in urging Congress to limit the size of the portfolio of Fannie and Freddie, which had grown from $136 billion in 1990 to $1.6 trillion in 2003, much of which was mortgage-backed securities.

In 2003 and 2004 major scandals engulfed both GSEs raising greater alarm about their management and government oversight. In June 2004 in response to the administrations criticisms about safety and soundness, seventy-six Democrats in the House sent a letter to President Bush supporting Fannie and Freddie and said any changes would likely negatively effect affordable housing goals. The signers included Nancy Pelosi, Barney Frank, Maxine Waters and Charlie Rangel.

Maxine Waters, "We should do no harm to these GSEs. We should be enhancing regulation, not making fundamental change. Mr. Chairman, we do not have a crisis at Freddie Mac and in particular at Fannie Mae under the outstanding leadership of Mr. Frank Raines. Everything has worked just fine under the 1997 Act."[6]

Barney Frank joined in, "I believe there has been more alarm raised about potential unsafety and unsoundness than in fact exists."

Several months later there was a wholesale replacement of senior management at both GSEs.

George Bush undoubtedly was concerned about his image as a wealthy Republican that didn't understand or perhaps care about the plight of working Americans, however his support of restraint and more effective regulation of Fannie and Freddie and at the same time expansion of homeownership was an impossible agenda.

The housing bubble burst on his watch just as it would have done if Bill Clinton were still president in 2008.

Chapter 27

Securitization

Although Robert Dall and Louis Ranieri at Salomon Brothers are generally recognized as the originators of the securitization of mortgage loans and later all kinds of consumer loans, securitization began in 1993 by a mortgage lender in Baton Rouge, Louisiana. United companies put together a pool of $165 million in mortgage loans and sold them to investors. The appeal was the three major rating agencies: Moody's, Standard & Poor and Fitch gave the pool of securities their highest rating: AAA.

United went on to bundle more loans and began venturing into below prime mortgage loans. In a short period of time United had sold $300 million mortgage-backed securities. It doesn't sound like a large number today, however no other company was doing it.

Fannie and Freddie were not allowed to own a mortgage underwriter and had to rely on banks and mortgage companies for product. Fannie and Freddie kept a watchful eye on any potential competitor and lenders did the same on the GSEs, opposing any attempt by Fannie and Freddie to gain authority to directly make mortgage loans.

Robert Dall was a senior bond trader at Salomon Brothers who thought of mortgage loans in an unconventional way. He thought if a loan could be sold as a bond the transaction would have to be structured so that it would be attractive to the seller and the buyer.

An investor would not be interested in a single bond or several bonds because the risk of default would be too concentrated, however if thousands of loans from around the country could be packaged, the risk would be spread and the interest stream attractive. It was the beginning of the enormous market in mortgage-backed securities.

Dall asked Louis Ranieri to join him in developing the securitization of mortgage loans. Ranieri was an aggressive rough guy who had worked his way up in the mail room to become head of the Utilities desk. The top bond traders are a unique breed and Ranieri was one of the best.

He came up with the idea of packaging loans into bundles which eventually became tranches (slices). In the initial stages Ranieri only dealt with prime mortgage loans. The various tranches could have different maturities.

An early problem in marketing was that the mortgage backed securities were not legal investments for municipal investment. Ranieri successfully lobbied for changes in the blue sky laws so the securities could be sold to state and local authorities.

He also convinced both Fannie and Freddie to guarantee the securities he was selling. It was an incredible performance how one man completely changed the mortgage market and consumer loan market, including credit cards, auto loans and just about every kind of consumer loan.

A former colleague of mine at State Street, Lowell Bryan, made a great observation when he was at McKinsey and Company. He said, "the force of securitization is unstoppable because it is driven by economics. As a nation, we should accept the fact that in the future anything that can be securitized will be securitized."[1]

Michael Lewis, a best-selling author and former Salomon Brothers bond trader, said Ranieri boasted that his trading desk at the height of Salomon's dominance in the mortgage trading market in 1984, made more than the rest of Wall Street combined."

Ranieri became Vice Chairman at Salomon and appeared to be the successor to John Gutfreund as CEO, but great success often comes at a price. Gutfreund apparently resented Ranieri's success and acclaim and fired him. Ranieri went on to other successful ventures but it was a sad ending for a genius who revolutionized the consumer loan market.

The traditional mortgage-back securities investor received a pro-rata share of principal and interest paid by the borrower each month. Larry Fink at the time was head of the mortgage trading desk at First Boston Corporation, (the investment bank not the commercial bank). Fink later went on to found the investment management firm Black Rock.

Fink also was a pioneer in mortgage bond-backed securities. He added an important feature to Ranieri's securities called a collateralized mortgage obligation (CMO). His CMO included a trust which is a legal entity that guarantees payments to the bondholders and could be registered with the SEC.

Most CMOs were given Fannie or Freddie-guarantees which made them investment-grade for bank capital requirements.

Roger Lowenstein wrote in 2010, "in the modern era no financial crisis erupted that did not have derivatives at its heart, beginning with the stock market crash of 1987 (Black Monday), in which derivatives instruments led the chain reaction selling. The leading troubadour was Alan Greenspan, who held that "regulation of derivative transactions that are privately negotiated by professionals is unnecessary."[2] The securitization of consumer loans brought with it an avalanche of new exotic financial instruments called derivatives. Although the term derivative has become part of our language the variety and complexity of derivatives make a simple definition difficult.

Basically, a derivative is a contract, the value of which derives from the underlying value of such assets as mortgages, stocks, bonds, and as many other things as an inventive mind on Wall Street can come up with.

Derivatives often were used to hedge a position that included two financial assets so that unfavorable price movement in one could be offset by a favorable movement in the other.

Securitization received a large expansion from the government in the early 1990s. The Financial Institutions Reform, Recovery and Enforcement Act of 1989. FIRREA was passed to bail out the failing savings and loan industry.

The Resolution Trust Corporation was part of the legislation. RTC took over $400 billion in distressed mortgages from failing savings and loans, many of the loans were high-risk loans. RTC bundled the loans, securitized them and sold them to the public.

Charles Gasparino reported, "by the end of the 1990s, the total value of credit derivatives was approaching $11 trillion, on its way to $100 trillion by the end of the decade. Bond derivatives were everywhere."[3]

Robert Citron, Treasurer of Orange County, California, used Merrill Lynch and Credit Suisse as investment advisers. Citron was a hero for making great returns for a number of years, however in the early 1990s interest rates began to rise and Citron bet heavily on fixed income derivatives and swaps. He and his advisers had made the wrong bets and Orange County declared bankruptcy in December, 1994. A number of lawsuits were filed and Citron spent a year in jail. Such was the mania taking over in all parts of the country.

In addition to mortgage-backed securities and collateralized mortgage obligations, there are several other types of derivatives that are important to the story.

Asset backed securities, ABS are bonds backed by mortgages but of lower quality than prime and not guaranteed by the GSEs.

Real Estate Mortgage Investment Conduits, REMICS, were issued directly by Fannie and Freddie as opposed to MBS which were pass throughs. Although REMICS are not mentioned very often, the OFHEO report in 2001 disclosed how a senior executive at Goldman Sachs advised Fannie how REMICS could be used to hide $107 million in profits to be used later if needed.

Structured Investment Vehicles, SIVS, are off-balance-sheet investments in subprime loans not generally rated. In 2007 the largest player in the SIV market was Citigroup. "Citigroup was the largest participant in the $350 billion SIV market, managing seven funds with a combined value of $80 billion."[4]

The attraction for Citi, in addition to enormous fees, was that the balance of the funds which Citi retained did not appear on the balance sheet and didn't require capital allocation.

In 2006 Citi had $1.8 trillion on its balance sheet but also another $ 2.1 trillion not on it's balance-sheet. Several federal regulations/examiners later acknowledged that they had never heard the term SIV.

The last derivative I will mention is the credit default swap, CDS, which Warren Buffet called a weapon of mass destruction.

A credit default swap is a contract that a buyer purchases as a form of insurance against the default of a bond or bundle of bonds or a loan or bundle of loans, ie. a bank could buy a CDS from AIG to protect against the loss on a loan.

A naked CDS is a swap someone can buy on an asset he does not own. Critics say that is like buying fire insurance on your neighbor's house. It gives you a perverse incentive to burn the house down. "The reason it's not illegal with CDSs is that no investor (other than the federal government) has enough clout to burn down houses by shorting mortgages."[5]

AIG, the largest insurance company in the world with 116,000 employees, offices in 116 countries and a leading seller of credit default swaps was in deep trouble in September 2008. The credit rating agencies downgraded AIG paper. The stock plunged 60% the next day. Lloyd Blankfein at Goldman Sachs had AIG contracts worth $20 billion.

By late 2007, AIG had sold CDS: totaling $440 billion. There was no exchange for trading CDS and it was literally impossible to determine the value.

As we know the government, meaning we the taxpayers, were called upon to bail out AIG, and by extension AIG customers.

Chapter 28

Freddie Scandal

Many of the books and articles written about the financial crisis mention Nassim Taleb's book, "The Black Swan, The Impact of the Highly Improbable." Taleb wrote about how highly intelligent people often fail to appreciate the randomness and unpredictability of human behavior and nature.

The title comes from English maritime history. When English sailors first arrived in Australia they were surprised to see black swans. All the swans in England where white.

The scandal at Freddie began in a black swan kind of way. In 2001, the Enron scandal involved their auditor Arthur Anderson, which at the time was one of the five major accounting firms. Enron eventually declared bankruptcy and Arthur Anderson was indicted for obstruction of justice.

Arthur Anderson had been Freddie's independent auditor for 31 years but it appeared it was time for Freddie to make a change in their auditors. Freddie moved to Price Waterhouse Cooper's, PWC.

Although Freddie had operated for years as Fannie's smaller twin, Freddie still enjoyed a special charter as a public/ private corporation beyond the reach of other publicly held corporations.

After Enron filed for bankruptcy and Arthur Andersen was indicted for obstruction of justice the Freddie directors announced in January, 2003 that they were delaying filing the company's financial results for the previous year, which is never good news. Freddie's auditor had questioned the company's accounting practices for the years 2000, 2001, 2002.

It was finally determined that Freddie had under-reported profits over the period by $4.5 billion. Under reporting sounds better then over-reporting profits, however it was a huge misstatement that had gone undetected for several years by Freddie's independent auditor and Freddie's regulator. Investors have every right to expect a company's financial results to be accurate.

The directors obviously where embarrassed and not happy; they hired Baker & Botts, a highly regarded law firm to conduct a thorough review of Freddie's financial management.

The directors, having lost confidence in their management team, fired David Glenn, President and Vaughn Clarke, Chief Financial Officer. Leland Brendsell, CEO, was allowed to resign. He received an exit package of $24 million plus retention of his stock options. Gary Parseghian, Chief Information Officer, was elected president.

The Office of Federal Housing Enterprise Oversight OFHEO, the reluctant regulator, decided to begin its own investigation. It was soon disclosed that Freddie's new President, Parseghian, was involved in a scheme to conceal $80 billion of derivatives used for hedging.

Just when one thought things couldn't get any worse, an OFHEO Report responded that management had been manipulating earnings for the sole purpose of paying executive bonuses. Parseghian was fired.

Freddie was drowning in bad news and at a critical time the directors made a final colossal mistake and hired Richard Syron, the former CEO of the Boston Fed to become the CEO of Freddie in December 2003.

It was Syron who gave us the seriously flawed mortgage study claiming widespread discrimination in mortgage lending in the Boston area in the early 1990s. Syron's leadership at Freddie was equally flawed.

Syron continued his crusade for easier mortgage approvals and he expanded Freddie's book of mortgage loans, mortgage-backed securities and guarantees. He also initiated a huge expansion in subprime loans. Immediately after joining Freddie he said his company was positioned to greatly increase its risk profile.

In mid 2004, Syron had been on board only six months when David Andrukonis, his Chief Risk Officer, warned him that "the procedures for purchasing or holding loans have become increasingly lax and expose the company and country to great financial risks."[1]

Syron ignored the warning and fired Andrukonis. Andrukonis went on to become a teacher.

Freddie was taken over by the government in September 2008 and Henry Paulson, Secretary of the Treasury, fired Richard Syron.

Charles Duhigg asked Syron in 2008 if he could have done something differently, Syron replied, "if I had better foresight maybe I could have improved things a little bit, but frankly if I had perfect foresight I would not have taken the job in the first place."

His cavalier remark about "improving things a little bit" was an insult to the American taxpayers who were on the hook for at least a 100-billion-dollar bailout.

Chapter 29

Fannie Explodes In Scandal

The rumors of the scandal at Freddie caused increasing concern among Fannie's directors in mid March 2003. They directed management to conduct a review of their financial affairs to make sure they didn't have problems similar to Freddie. It's unbelievable that management submitted its report to the Board of Directors and claimed that any problems at the company were minor or immaterial. The report was later described as misleading when in fact it was blatantly dishonest.

As word leaked out about the board's concerns, Rains went into damage control. He gave interviews and made public statements. In June 2003 he said, "Everyone who has looked at it from our external auditors to our regulators found we are doing this in a state-of-the-art way. We are compulsive about risk."[1]

Armando Falcon (at OFHEO) who was embarrassed for missing the $4.5 billion accounting problem at Freddie, adopted an aggressive concern and asked Congress for a substantial increase in his budget to conduct an investigation. George Bush recommended an increase in the OFHEO budget from $40 million to $59 million.

Falcon began a special examination in late 2003 and in the spring, realizing he would be confronted with an all-out assault from Fannie's friends in Congress he hired Deloitte & Touche to lead the examination.

Falcon's interim report disclosed improper mismanagement of financial results. Especially troubling was that much of the improper accounting was used to reach earnings per-share target to pay executive bonuses.

It was not unusual for Fannie to regularly reach earnings-per-share targets within a dollar. The EPS goal for 1998 was $2.48, earnings came in at $2.476.

The report also contained details of Raine's compensation from 1998 through 2003; he received more than $90 million,more than half of which was from bonus awards. In 1998, Fannie recorded low income housing credits to reach the bonus goal. Five hundred and forty seven people including Raines shared in a $27.1 million pool.

The Security and Exchange Commission soon joined in the investigation of Fannie. The SEC requested a meeting with officials from OFHEO and Fannie. Donald Nicolaisen, Chief SEC Accountant, told the group that Raine's claim that Fannie had state-of-the-art accounting was so far out of bounds it was from another planet. Fannie Mae was coming apart at the seams and Raines did not have any response. He retired shortly after.

The Fannie directors must have had a terrible feeling of betrayal and embarrassment. They formed a Special Review Committee (SRC) and retained Paul, Weiss, Rifkind, Wharton and Garrison, LLP. They also retained former Senator Warren Rudman as Special Counsel. The forensic accounting firm Huron Consulting Group became part of the team.

Paul Weiss et al examined more than four million pages of hard copy and electronic documents and conducted 240 interviews. The Executive Summary was over thirty pages long. The report supported the findings of OFHEO.

The following is a brief example of some of the findings:

"The information management provided the directors with respect to accounting, financial reporting and internal audit issues generally was unacceptable and at times misleading."

Office of the chairman...."The actual corporate culture suffered from an attitude of arrogance (both internally and externally) and discouraged dissenting views, criticism and bad news."

Accounting, "Management accounting practices in virtually all areas were not consistent with generally accepted accounting practices."

Employees, "Employees who occupied critical accounting, financial reporting and audit functions were either unqualified for their position or did not understand their roles or failed to carry out their roles."

Raines and Timothy Howard, Chief Financial Officer and Leanne Spencer, Controller, were fined $110 million for alleged abuses. The charges were settled out of court for $31 million, a large portion of which were stock options of little value. The Wall Street Journal estimated that Fannie's insurance company paid a large part of the penalty.

In spite of the growing scandals at Fannie and Freddie the usual members of Congress rallied to defend both companies in hearings and public statements.

One of the most outspoken and disgraceful was Senator Kit Bond, a Republican from Missouri. He was one of the largest recipients of contributions from Fannie and Freddie.

Bond attempted to intimidate and interfere with the officials at OFHEO from conducting their government responsibility in investigating Fannie. Bond sent a letter to the Inspector General at HUD and asked for an investigation of the persons at OFHEO who were investigating Fannie.

Fortunately there was no response to Bond's letter, however Gretchen Morgenson and Joshua Rosner reported that a draft of Bond's letter was later found on a Fannie Mae computer two weeks before it was sent.[2]

Bond didn't give up trying to interfere with OFHEO. He tried to slip in language to defund unless Falcon was removed but that didn't work either.

Bond was not the only Republican who received generous contributions from Fannie and Freddie; an article in the Salt Lake Tribune described Senator Robert Bennett from Utah as follows, "few politicians have more ties to Fannie and Freddie then Utah Sen. Bob Bennett, who topped all Republicans in campaign contributions from the duo since 1999. Bennett received $107,999 in contributions from executives at the two companies. Only three members of Congress, all Democrats, received more, Chris Dodd, presidential candidate Barack Obama and Sen. John Kerry."[3]

Michael Oxley, Republican congressman from Ohio, was Chairman of the House Financial Services Committee in 2000. He refused to support Richard Baker's reform legislation. Freddie held 40 fundraisers for Oxley.

Ed Royce, Republican from California,, also refused to support the Baker legislation. Robert Ney, Republican from Ohio, also refused. Ney later was found guilty in a lobbying scandal.

Chapter 30

The Government Sponsored Enterprise Act

Although Fannie and Freddie performed their missions admirably for many years fundamental changes were made in 1992 with the passage of the Federal Safety and Soundness Act generally known as the GSE Act. The full name is the Federal Housing Enterprises Financial Safety and Soundness Act of 1992.

Henry Gonzalez, of Texas, the powerful Chairman of the House Banking Committee, a liberal Democrat, had the original Safety and Soundness Bill withdrawn to give legislators more time to study the issues. The delay also gave ACORN, with Gonzalez's invitation, participation in writing the rules that would allow Fannie and Freddie to purchase loans with fewer traditional requirements. Fannie executives also were given the opportunity to assist in writing the legislation.

The Act unfortunately split the regulatory structure of the two companies. It gave HUD general regulatory authority in all areas of operations except safety and soundness.

The Secretary of Housing and Urban Development, HUD, for the first time was given authority to set housing goals and monitor compliance. It was a major expansion of authority for HUD and began the destruction of Fannie Mae and Freddie Mac.

Initially the law required 30 per cent of housing units financed by Fannie and Freddie should go to low and moderate income families and another 30 per cent should provide housing in the inner cities. These goals would be steadily increased.

The second part of the law regarding regulatory structure created the Office of Federal Housing Enterprise Oversight, OFHEO, to oversee the financial safety and soundness of the two companies. Splitting authority generally is not a good practice, but it's likely James Johnson had a hand in it to make sure OFHEO would be a weak regulator. Johnson was skillful in making sure that Fannie really answered to Congress and not any federal regulators.

The GSE Act also required the Treasury to complete several tests of the GSEs by December 1994. The report included tests for capital adequacy, stress tests and recommendations on whether the two companies should be privatized and whether some or all of the special benefits they enjoyed should be discontinued.

It was a formidable task and it's probably not surprising that the Treasury had not filed any of the required reports by early 1996. However, there was speculation that a report on privatization was in the works.

It's known that Robert Rubin, Secretary of the Treasury and Larry Summers, Deputy Secretary, were not pleased with what their colleagues had written and they had the report rewritten. The rewritten report recommended virtually no changes.

James Johnson, CEO of Fannie, spent $1.9 million in the first six months of 1996 in lobbying members of Congress. The executives at Fannie and Freddie celebrated another victory, but the battle was not over. The Congressional Budget Office was asked to review the same issues.

Unfortunately, there are too few heroes in the Fannie and Freddie saga. Gretchen Morgenson and Joshua Rosen deserve a lot of credit for telling the story of June O'Neil, Head of CBO and Marvin Phaup, Deputy CBO in their book, "Reckless Endangerment." It's a good story about two honest government officials who stood their ground and refused to be bullied by other powerful members of the government and some members of the media.

Congressman Richard Baker, Republican from Louisiana, Chairman of the Financial Services Subcommittee, held hearings in 1996 to review the CBO report. The executives at Fannie and Freddie had continually preached that all the special benefits received by the companies because of their government affiliation were passed on to the borrowers; that assertion was about to be severely challenged.

Marvin Phaup began the study in 1995 to determine two things: the amount of subsidies Fannie and Freddie received as a result of the implied governance guarantee and how much was passed on to the borrowers.

Director O'Neil was accompanied by Phaup to the Baker hearing. Director O'Neil gave an overview of the report and its recommendation. In spite of Baker's efforts to maintain civility both O'Neil and Phaup where assaulted brutally and even personally about their competence.

Congressman Baker also was attacked as anti-home ownership and anti-minorities. After he left Congress he said that the arrogance exhibited by Fannie and Freddie has never been exhibited by that kind of political power.

Phaup's report outlined how Fannie and Freddie received approximately $6.5 billion annually in government benefits. The Treasury using different assumptions pegged the number at $ 5.3 billion.

This CBO report found that in 1995, the GSEs made $4.4 billion available to borrowers, but $2.1 billion went to fund executive bonuses and dividends. Five executives received $44 million in stock options that year.

The implied government guarantee allowed the two companies to sell billions of dollars in bonds in the US and around the world at rates slightly above treasuries. Both companies had a $2.25 billion line of credit from the Treasury which gave them borrowing rates substantially below market rates.

They were allowed to operate with minimum amounts of capital and maximum leverage and both were exempt from taxes, including real estate taxes. The CBO report concluded that the benefits they received were an extremely costly way to help homeowners that would justify more than $2 billion annually, as a "retained tax-payer subsidy."

Although President Bush supported congressman Baker's bill (HR3703) in the end Michael Oxley, the Republican Chairman of the House Finance Committee refused to support Baker, his subcommittee chairman. Ed Royce, Republican from California, and Robert Ney, Republican from Ohio also refused support. Twenty-five members of Baker's committee were flooded with contributions from Fannie and Freddie. The bill died in committee.

Fannie and Freddie had once again derailed any attempt at legislation to strengthen government regulation and oversight. Daniel Mudd, the last CEO of Fannie before the government takeover summed it up very well when he said, "The old political reality was we always won, we took no prisoners and we faced little organized political opposition."

The celebration was brief. A few years down the road, Fannie and Freddie were engulfed in scandals.

Chapter 31

The Repeal Of The Glass-Steagall Act

The politicians who were most involved in the financial crisis have attempted to cover up their role by blaming George Bush for banking deregulation during his term in office. Sen. Chris Dodd and Congressman Barney Frank blamed Bush and they also blamed the banking regulators for their failure to rein in Fannie and Freddie, in spite of the fact that there was no significant deregulation of banking during the Bush years and both Dodd and Frank were the two members of Congress that vigorously supported less regulation for Fannie and Freddie.

Two major banking laws were passed during Bill Clinton's presidency: the repeal of the Glass-Steagall Act and the Riegel-Neal Interstate Banking Act. The repeal legislation of the Glass-Steagall Act known as the Gramm, Leach, Bliley Act of 1999 or GBL, or the formal name, the Financial Services Modernization Act, was sponsored by Senator Phil Gramm from Texas and Congressmen Jim Leach from Iowa and Tom Bliley from Virginia. The Act eliminated the prohibition on combining commercial banking and investment banking.

There had been several previous attempts over the years to repeal Glass-Steagall that required the separation of commercial banking investment banking but none was successful; however it probably was inevitable that some erosion would take place over the course of 65 years after the Depression.

In my early days in banking a list of the hundred largest banks in the world would have been almost entirely U.S. banks. As England, Europe and Japan recovered from the ravages of war the list increasingly included banks from outside the US.

The playing field began to tilt a little because foreign banks now doing business in the U.S. could underwrite long-term bond issues and stock issues in their countries but U.S. banks could not do so here.

The Fed granted limited authority to allow banks to underwrite commercial paper and municipal revenue bonds. In January, 1989, corporate bonds were added; the dam had been breached. Then Sandy Weill and Citigroup successfully violated the law.

The second banking deregulation law passed during the Clinton presidency was the Reigle-Neal Interstate Banking and Branching Efficiency Act 1994, which permitted interstate banking. Both GBL and Reigle-Neal were ground breaking legislation.

The Glass-Steagall Act 1933 was passed during the Depression and signed into law by President Roosevelt. The law was passed to reduce concentration in banking and excessive risk-taking by separating commercial banking and investment banking. The law also created the FDIC.

All of the investment banks that were affiliated with commercial banks were spun off as private partnerships. First Boston was an exception. It became an independent shareholder company.

First Boston subsequently entered a joint venture with Credit Suisse (1978) and later ran into financial troubles causing Credit Suisse to acquire controlling interest in the company in violation of the law. The Fed decided the deal was preferable to a bankruptcy and looked the other way.

A major structural change in the investment business began in 1971 when Merrill Lynch went public. Salomon Brothers followed in 1978, Bear Stearns and Morgan Stanley a few years later and Lehman Brothers in 1994 and Goldman Sachs in 1999. The reason given for going public was the need to raise capital to compete with the international banks that were doing business in the U.S.

John Gillespie, a former investment banker said, "the shift to public ownership also replaced the accountability of partnerships -- when there are no profits, there are no bonuses -- these public companies had board members who either weren't paying attention - or Lehman in particular - were deliberately selected because they were unqualified or out of it."[1]

Gillespie could have added there is a long history of directors being selected as payback for past favors. Fannie and Freddie are good examples.

The calls to bring back Glass—Steagall and break up the big banks like Citi, Bank of America, J.P. Morgan Chase and Wells Fargo generally do not include an idea how to recapitalize the spinoffs or what to do about the foreign banks in this country like Barclays, Credit Suisse, Deutsche Bank and UBS.

Sandy Weill began his career at Bear Stearns which he left after an uneventful period to start his own company with several friends. In a period of years he assumed the chairmanship and began the acquisition of a number of companies. In 1980, his company Shearson Loeb Rhodes had capital of $280 million and was second to Merrill Lynch in the securities brokerage business.

Weill then sold the business to American Express; however it was predictable that James Robinson III and Weill, both with outsized egos, would have problems working together. Weill decided to leave and he asked Jamie Dimon to join him. Although Dimon had a good relationship with Robinson he decided to take his chances with Weill.

Weill made a move to take over Bank of America that was turned down, he was then approached by Commercial Credit for a buyout. "Commercial Credit had combined in an unlikely combination with Control Data. Weill invested $6 million and Dimon $425,000 to do the deal."[2]

Weill and Dimon embarked on whirlwind acquisitions sprees to buy more than a hundred companies, including Primerica, the parent company of Smith Barney for $1.65 billion and the acquisition of their old company, American Express for $1.2 billion. They completed a huge acquisition of Travelers Insurance for $4 billion. Weill renamed their company Travelers Group.

In 1998, Weill made a mega-deal that combined Travelers with Citicorp to become Citigroup. There was, however, a problem. The combination of Travelers Group and Citi was in direct violation of the Glass—Steagall Act In a stunning development Dimon was not included as a director in the new board. In fact as President he had only one direct report, Heidi Miller, CFO. The writing was on the wall. Weill fired Dimon..

Dimon was out and he was very mad. He left New York to become Chief Executive of Banc One in Ohio, but he would be back.

Weill had his super financial store in place; Citigroup operated in a hundred countries with 22,000 offices and almost 400,000 employees. Weill had a hundred million customers. Citigroup was the biggest, but still in violation of the law. Citigroup was granted a forbearance agreement for two years on the assumption the law would be changed. Any company granted such an exception to a federal law had to have a lot of connections; sheer size was not enough.

Robert Rubin was Bill Clinton's Secretary of the Treasury and he gave his full support to repeal of the Glass-Steagall act with one major caveat: any banking organization would not receive federal approval to enter a merger or acquisition if it had not received a satisfactory CRA rating in a recent examination. Clinton joined and threatened to veto any bill without the CRA provision.

Rubin worked with Gramm and his republican colleagues on the GBL legislation with the CRA provision. He said, "I care greatly about CRA."

President Clinton signed the act a few weeks before he left office. Rubin also left and joined Citi in a rather unusual position described as a "three-person office of the chairman." The three were Weill and John Reed, who were co-presidents, and Rubin. Rubin had no direct responsibilities, however he was a Director and Chairman of the Executive Committee.

Reed had been the visionary at Citi Corp in developing its huge worldwide retail business; presumably he had a good relationship with his board of directors, but one might anticipate being a co-president with Sandy Weill would require a bodyguard.

Weill enlisted Rubin in the effort to convince the board the company should have only one chief executive officer which of course was himself.

Rubin was able to convince Michael Armstrong, CEO of AT&T and Citi Director to support Weill in ousting Reed. It was not long before he resigned.

Weill had achieved everything he wanted in business. He stood at the top of the world, but it was about to end badly for him.

The story has been told a number of times. Basically Weill asked Jack Grubman, a security analyst, to upgrade his rating on AT&T and in return Weill agreed to help Grubman's daughter get into an exclusive private school where Weill was a trustee.

Eliot Spitzer, the Attorney General, became aware of emails regarding the deal and threatened to bring fraud charges against Weill and Citigroup.

Charles "Chuck" Prince, Citigroup's legal counsel, negotiated a deal with Spitzer for Weill to step down from any active role at Citi. Weill escaped personal penalties but Citi paid a $400 million fine.

Rubin was asked to assume a more active role as chairman which he did for almost two years before resigning in 2009. During his tenure at Citigroup his annual compensation was in the range of $15 million.

Chuck Prince, an outstanding lawyer took over running Citigroup, but he had an extremely short period of time to get his hands around the largest financial institution in the world.

He made an odd statement that was quoted in the Financial Times in July 2007. He said, "When the music stops in terms of liquidity things will be complicated. But as long as the music is playing, you've got to get up and dance. We're still dancing."

It didn't go over well with some of his shareholders; the company that had a market capitalization of $400 billion was stuck at $45 per share.

There is an unbelievable story that apparently is true. Prince learned for the first time at a board meeting that his bank had $45 billion in various mortgage securities on its books. Prince asked his associate who gave the report if he anticipated any losses and he was assured no losses were likely.

Two months later losses were estimated to be in the range of $10 billion. Losses began to increase rapidly and Prince agreed to step down in November 2007. He left with a generous separation package.

Chuck Prince was succeeded by Vikram Pandit who was handpicked by Rubin. Pandit was a university professor early in his career but he left the academic world to join Morgan Stanley. Sheila Bair, the former FDIC Chairman, wrote that "he was forced out in 2005 and started his own hedge fund, Old Lane Partners, which delivered break even performance. In July 2007, Citigroup purchased the fund for $800 million. Pandit had reaped at least $165 million out of the deal. He was named CEO of Citi in early 2007… A few months later the fund was closed."[3]

Roger Lowenstein had an interesting comment about Pandit's leadership of a sinking ship. Lowenstein wrote, "Well into the crisis., when banks such as Citigroup were operating on federal investment and Citi stock was in single digits, Vikram Pandit, the CEO, was observed with a lunch guest at Le Bernardin the top-rated restaurant in New York…Pandit ordered a $350 bottle of wine so that, as he explained, he could savor a glass of wine worth drinking. Pandit had one glass, his friend had none."[4]

Back at the office where his colleagues were worried about their future and the downsizing of Citi such things rarely go unnoticed. Citi had 357,000 employees in 2007. By the first quarter of 2013 the number was down to 260,000, a drop of 27 per cent. Before Pandit stepped down he announced another 11,000 employee reduction in the coming months.

Ten years earlier Sandy Weill and Robert Rubin were lobbying for banking deregulation and now the taxpayers owned 36 percent of the giant in preferred shares.

Chapter 32

Commodities Futures
Trading Commission

The original Commodity Exchange Act of 1936 applied to agricultural commodities like corn, wheat and pork bellies, all of which were regulated by the Chicago Board of Trade. The law was updated in 1974 to create the Commodity Futures Trading Commission, CFTC, as the new regulator. Derivatives, however, were well down the road.

President Clinton appointed a commission in 1999 known as the President's Working group. It included Larry Summers, Deputy Secretary Treasury; Alan Greenspan, Chairman of the Fed; Arthur Leavitt, Chairman of the SEC, and William Rainer, Chair of the CFTC.

The group designed the Commodity Futures Modernization Act of 2000. The bill was debated for a short period of time and received Clinton's support. It seemed there would be a quick passage, but Senator Phil Gramm, the powerful Republican from Texas who chaired the Banking Committee, insisted that the bill not contain any regulations pertaining to credit default swaps, which at the time totaled about $80 trillion. Credit Default Swaps, (CDS) at the time were exempt from most federal regulation.

Brooksley Born was named the new head of the CFTC. She had an impressive background. She was elected president of the Stanford Law Review in 1963, the first woman to hold that prestigious position and she went on to become a highly regarded lawyer. She was later appointed as one of the commissioners on the Financial Crisis Inquiry Commission.

There was an ongoing and sometimes acrimonious debate between her agency and the Securities and Exchange Commissioner about how credit default swaps should be regulated. Born wrote a "draft report" which drew immediate criticism from Robert Rubin, Larry Summers and Arthur Leavitt.

Summers "demanded she not release the report and yelled there are thirteen bankers in my office that say if it is published we will have the worst financial crisis since World War II."

Rubin, who generally was polite, joined in and rudely "asked if she would like an education in the law from the Treasury's General Counsel."[1]

Born was threatened with legislation to prevent her releasing the report or issuing new regulations. She published her "draft report" anyway. She resigned from the CFTC shortly after.

The Commodity Futures Modernization Act was introduced on December 15, 2000, the last day before the Christmas recess. It was not debated in the Senate or House and was attached to a 1100 page omnibus budget bill. President Clinton signed the bill on his last day in office.

It was a truly odious piece of legislation; there was a section known as the Enron loophole that specifically exempted credit default swaps from CFTC regulations.

It's not a coincidence, perhaps, that Dr. Wendy Gramm, Senator Gramm's wife, who had a PhD in economics and was former chair of the CFTC and current member of Enron, was a major recipient of Enron contributions.

According to Barry Ritholtz, Dr. Gramm was paid, "between $915,000 and $1.85 million in salary, attendance fees, stock options sales and dividends from 1993 to 2001. The value of Wendy Gramm's Enron stock options swell from no more than $1500 in 1995 to as much as $500,000 by 2000."[2]

Sen. Phil Gramm was one of the largest recipients of contributions from Enron.

Enron filed for bankruptcy in 2001 and a criminal investigation revealed internal documents which show that Enron executives were involved in writing the Commodity Futures Modernization Act.

Chapter 33

Mark To Market

The term quants became part of our language in the early 1990s. It was used to describe a new breed of math wizards that were developing extremely complex computer models using risk programs and mathematics-based investments strategies to predict how financial markets work. The models were supposed to predict human behavior within a very narrow range.

A group of young J.P. Morgan financial experts met in Boca Raton, Florida, in the mid-1990s. It was an intense meeting but also a wild one fueled by a lot of alcohol and partying. Participants were thrown in the pool, along with furniture, and there was at least one broken nose.

The task they had undertaken was to develop a computer model that would measure the daily volatility of the banks positions and then translate that volatility into a dollar amount. It was a monumental task!

In spite of the partying and perhaps because of it, the J.P. Morgan Quants developed a model called value-at-risk, VAR.

VAR was designed to calculate the amount of value a user could lose over a 24 hour period with a 95 percent probability. If the model worked with the assumed degree of certainty, then any investment risk could be managed by hedging strategies.

In December 1997, the J.P. Morgan Quants unveiled its new model called Bistro. Scott Patterson wrote in his book, "The Quants" "The first Bistro deal allowed J.P. Morgan to unload nearly $1 billion in credit risk from its balance sheet."[1]

The J.P. Morgan Quants had been working on the problem for many years. The problem was the huge inventory of loans on the bank's balance sheet that was earning low returns and requiring capital reserve.

The credit default swap, CDS, was created in the early 1990s. A CDS basically was a contract that provided insurance in the event of default on a bond or bundle of bonds. The price of the insurance reflected the riskiness of the bonds.

A collateralized debt obligation, CDO, was a bundle of securities, mortgages, consumer loans, sliced into various levels of risk.

The J. P. Morgan Quants introduced a truly bizarre product: the synthetic CDO. Scott Patterson wrote, "The bank came up with a novel idea of creating a synthetic CDO using swaps. The swaps were tied to the loans that had been sitting on J. P. Morgan's balance sheet, repackaged into a CDO. Investors, instead of buying an actual bundle of bonds - getting the yield on the bonds, but assuming the risk of default - were instead agreeing to insure a bundle of bonds, getting a premium to do so."[2]

J. P. Morgan and other banks continued to off-load billions of dollars of risk from their balance sheets to investors through collateralized debt obligations to free up capital for additional lending. All of this contributed to the credit freeze of 2007 and 2008.

John Meriwether who was a rising star at Salomon Brothers, left to start his own hedge fund, Long Term Capital Management, LTCM, in 1993. He brought with him a number of his former colleagues at Salomon Brothers plus future Noble prize winners Myron Scholes and Robert Merton as directors. LTCM started trading with $1 billion in investor capital.

A simple description of an extremely complex business was LTCM specialized in relative-value opportunities. They looked for relationships between securities that were out of whack. Meriwether and his company invested $20 million in the J.P. Morgan risk model.

Meriwether had a great run for a period of years, producing huge returns for his partners. LTCM operated at high levels of leverage and they were borrowing up to $125 million per day from commercial banks and Wall Street investment banks.

Then a "Black Swan" suddenly and unexpectedly showed up. Russia defaulted on it's debt in August 1998. Meriwether's company lost $550 million in a single day on August 21.

By the end of August the company had burned through $2 billion of the $4.8 billion of investor capital. The company desperately needed as much as $1.5 billion in new capital. Warren Buffett and Jon Corzine at Goldman Sachs were rumored to be potential saviors, but neither worked out.

There was great concern at the Fed about the huge amount of debt that LTCM owed U.S. and foreign banks. The New York Fed put together a consortium of banks and investment banks to bail out LTCM in September. It was the first time the Fed had bailed out a non-depository institution. The 14 banks contributed $3.6 billion and in exchange they received 90 percent of John Meriwether's company.

The financial companies at the time valued their inventories of mortgage-backed securities and other securities according to programs like VAR or their own models developed or adapted by their risk managers and investment people. Most of the models used entry prices of the securities purchased. It is known as mark to model.

In spite of the collapse of Long Term Capital Management the SEC continued to allow the big banks to use mark to model. As the markets began to weaken, especially for mortgage-backed securities, the Financial Accounting Standards Board, FASB, known as faz-bee issued FAZ 157 to take effect November, 2007. The ruling could not have come at a worse time.

FAZ 157 states, "the changes to current practice resulting from the application of this statement relates to the definition of fair value, the methods used to measure fair value and expand disclosures about fair value measurements." It also stated that fair value should include an adjustment for risk... and it is based on exit price and not entry price. FAZ 157 meant that such investments should be marked to market.

FAZ 157 did allow for suspension of the mark to market rule if there was no active market, however, the SEC ignored all pleas for relief, even temporary relief, until October 30, 2008, when it finally agreed there was no active market for mortgage-backed securities and suspended the rule.

It was a month too late to save AIG, the world's largest insurance company. It was also too late to save Lehman Brothers, one of the oldest and largest investment banks. Fannie and Freddie didn't get a pass. Billions of dollars of capital were extinguished and we plunged deeper into the worst recession since the Depression.

Economists Brian Wesbury and Robert Stein wrote in Forbes on February 24, 2009, "Two things are absolutely essential when fixing financial market problems: time and growth. Time to work things out and growth to make working those things out easier. Mark to market accounting takes both of these things away."

The mark to market rule is not a new problem. During the Depression when the banks were failing all over the country President Roosevelt suspended the rule in 1938. Incidentally, the Federal Reserve does not mark to market billions of dollars it has on the books including hundreds of billions in mortgage-backed securities. Losses are only recognized when securities are sold at a loss.

I ran into the problem years ago when I was at Bank of New Hampshire. Our accounting firm decided we should mark to market our government bond portfolio. We used a very conservative investment policy called laddered maturities. The portfolio had short-term, medium-term and long-term bonds. When the long-term bonds matured the funds were rolled into the short-term section.

My argument was we did not actively trade government securities and never took losses. Eventually it was agreed that government securities where the safest investments in the world and as long as we didn't engage in a trading policy there was no need to mark the securities to market each quarter.

Although the suspension of the rule should have been implemented much earlier which would have prevented the loss of some of the capital that was wiped out and replaced by TARP funds, it is clear that many of the largest banks and investment houses did not have a good idea of the value of their investment portfolios even in good times.

AIG Financial Products Division, was part of American International Group. It was started in 1987, many of the officers were former associates of Michael Milken at Drexel Burnham, including Howard Sosin who ran the division. Sosin claimed to have a better model to trade interest rate swaps.

Sosin's group was hugely profitable every year for 15 years. There was no evidence of trouble on the horizon. Michael Lewis reported that Howard Sosin took nearly $200 million with him when he left.

Sosin was replaced by Joe Cassano who also produced huge profits for AIG. AIG continued to write credit default swaps to insure piles of loans but now had moved from insuring loans for companies like IBM & GE. AIG was insuring just about anything that came down the pike.

Michael Lewis told the following story in his best-selling book, "The Big Shot," Cassano's associate, Gene Park, had warned earlier that an increase in homeowner default would put in enormous strain on AIG's capital. His warning was not only rejected, but Cassano screamed at him saying he did not know what he was talking about.

In 2005 Park decided to analyze the loans AIG was insuring through credit default swaps. After his initial work he called Gary Gordon, a Yale professor, who developed the model that AIG FP was using to price credit default swaps. "Gorton guessed that the piles were no more than 10 percent subprime. Park then asked a risk analyst in London the same question, he guessed 20 percent. None of them knew it was 95 percent, said one trader. and I'm sure Cassano didn't know either."

After AIG received $85 billion from the Fed, the Treasury provided another $100 billion.

Bank of America was anxious to close the deal to acquire Merrill Lynch and the government also was pushing the deal. There was virtually no market for buying or selling mortgage-backed securities. Merrill Lynch sold $30 billion in mortgage backed securities for 22 cents on the dollar. The securities may not have been worth book value based on cash flow but given time it's likely the price would have been more than 22 cents.

The Bank of America deal to acquire Merrill Lynch had a great effect on the market. Large fire sales generally lead to more fire sales further pushing the market down. The value of mortgage-backed securities held in pension plans, mutual funds, 401(k)s, private investments and by Fannie and Freddie worth over $7 trillion in the United States and around the world suddenly became uncertain.

Chapter 34

March 2008: The Panic Begins

The financial crisis began in March 2008 when Bear Stearns, the fifth largest investment bank, but one of the smallest, was acquired by J.P. Morgan Chase. Bear Stearns had been in business since 1923.

Bear had to borrow as much as $10 billion every day to conduct business, however, there was growing concern about the value of Bear's mortgage backed securities for collateral. Bear's problems were exacerbated by negative rumors and short sellers.

Bear had taken a big hit to its reputation in July the previous year when two of its major funds filed for bankruptcy. High Grade Structured Credit Fund, (note the name), resulted in a loss of $900 million for many of Bear's customers. High Grade Enhanced Leverage Fund lost $600 million. The total loss of $1.5 billion was a serious black eye.

Bear was on the brink of failure in March 2008, Timothy Geithner, President of the New York Fed, offered Jamie Dimon at J.P. Morgan Chase a $30 billion line of credit to acquire Bear Stearns.

Jamie Dimon offered to acquire Bear for two dollars per share, a few weeks earlier the stock was selling for over $60 per share. A Bear employee said the price of $236 million was less than the value of their headquarters on Madison Avenue. There were complaints that Bear should have been given access to the Discount Window.

Subsequently it was found that Bear Energy, a little-known subsidiary, had $1.6 billion of unrealized gains on commodity prices on its books. The final price for the acquisition was raised to $10 per share.

Bill Bamber, a Senior Managing Director at Bear, who lost his job and a large chunk of his wealth said the following about Alan Schwartz "the CEO who went down with the ship, was offered the position of non-executive vice chairman at J.P. Morgan. True to the person that he is and will always be in my mind, Alan declined the offer; he felt it wouldn't be fair to the several thousand former Bear employees who hadn't been offered jobs with J.P. They don't make them like that anymore."[1]

Among the villains there were some heroes.

Henry Paulson, Secretary of the Treasury, briefed President Bush on the growing financial crisis and described a bold "plan to use Fannie and Freddie to buy more mortgage securities as means of helping hard-pressed banks."[2] Two days later the deal was announced. OFHEO would let the twins stretch their capital by investing 200 billion more in housing.

Fannie and Freddie were six months away from insolvency and anyone close to the scene had to know that the two GSE's were burning through very thin capital and not the best choice to rescue Wall Street.

In July 2008 the Fed issued an upbeat statement from the recent meeting of the Federal Open Market Committee (FOMC) meeting. It said, "the economy is expected to expand slowly over the rest of the year. FOMC participants anticipate a gradual strengthening of economic growth over the coming months."

Although Bernanke and the board members may have been trying to strike a positive note, they of course should not have misled the public. They had to know subprime loans were showing higher delinquencies. Something else was happening that had not happened in decades, house prices were falling sharply.

There was another alarming sign. IndyMac Bank in Pasadena, California, was placed into receivership by the FDIC on July 11, 2008. For the first time in 70 years we witnessed an old-time bank-run pictures of long lines of depositors waiting to withdraw their funds. There was great concern another such event could cause a collapse of the entire banking system.

The FDIC had not faced the challenge of dealing with multiple bank failures in recent times. Sheila Bair, Chairman of the FDIC, would lock horns with Henry Paulson, Ben Bernanke, Tim Geithner and John Dugan many times in the months ahead over the role of the FDIC in the Financial Crisis.

During and after the crisis we kept hearing the terms, interconnectedness, systemic consequences and "Too Big To Fail". The role of complex derivatives played a major role in the Financial Crisis, but Too Big to Fail and interconnectedness is really not something new in the banking world.

There were two bank failures in the 1980s, Penn Square and Continental Illinois, that we should have learned from.

Penn Square bank was located in a shopping mall in Oklahoma City. It was not, however, a small retail bank. Pen Square was a high flier with 80% of its loans in oil and gas leases. The deposit base was only $500 million, but it made billions of dollars in energy related loans. It was able to do such a large volume of loans by participating most of each loan to other banks. Continental Illinois was a major participant with over $1 billion in energy loans.

Penn Square was profitable for everyone for a while but as generally happens the boom time ended when oil and gas prices declined. Suddenly Penn Square was on the verge of failure.

The Federal Reserve, the OCC and the FDIC couldn't agree on a resolution. William Isaac, Chairman of the FDIC wanted to payoff the deposits up to the hundred thousand dollars insured limit. All the investors, which included banks, credit unions and money funds would take major losses.

Paul Volcker, Fed Chairman, tried to get other banks to join in a rescue but was unsuccessful. Eventually the Comptroller of the Currency placed Penn Square into receivership and losses were significant.

It might have been the end of the story but Continental Illinois, the seventh largest bank in the country, was injured and there was growing concern about Continental's exposure to energy loans. Roger Anderson, CEO, was an aggressive lender and not only did he participate in large energy loans from Penn Square, he made huge bets on a Louisiana oil and gas company.

Continental was known as the "Morgan of the West" with deposit accounts from over 2000 correspondent banks.

At the time banks in Illinois were restricted to one office. Continental had a 23 story tower connected by an aerial bridge to a second tower to comply with the law.

In spite of the substantial business connections Continental's core deposit base was only $4 billion with assets in excess of $40 billion. The assets were supported by short-term borrowing in certificates of deposits, Eurodollars, and commercial paper.

As soon as the good times stopped Continental was in trouble. In 1982 Paul Volcker gave Anderson and the directors a blunt warning about their excessive risk-taking. The warning was delivered in Volcker's office and was serious business. Anderson ignored the warning and continued business as usual.

In 1984, just two years later, Continental failed. The Fed fearing a chain reaction provided $9 billion in loans and a group of large banks provided another $4.7 billion in backup loans with FDIC guarantees.

Stuart McKinney, a maverick Republican congressman from Connecticut, who served 8 terms in an overwhelmingly Democratic district, popularized the phrase "Too Big to Fail" in conjunction with the bailout of Continental.

History has shown that even the most confident and highly regarded chairman of the Federal Reserve have been reluctant to use their authority to take timely and decisive actions to curtail a rogue bank. Paul Volcker delivered the warning to Roger Anderson and company at Continental but he did not follow up with further actions like a 'cease and desist order" when his caution was ignored.

The Home Ownership and Equity Protection Act of 1994 (HOEPA) was sponsored by Representative Joe Kennedy and signed into law by President Clinton. It was primarily directed at the deceptive mortgage lending practices, but it also gives the Fed broad powers to set bank and non-bank mortgage lending standards.

The Fed had the authority to prevent much of the abuse and recklessness that led to the housing collapse. The Fed was the only government agency with the authority to set the standards across the board for all mortgage lenders.

The Fed chairman often served longer terms than their counterparts at the treasury who generally serve concurrently with the president who appointed them. The following is a list of Fed chairman going back to 1951:

William McChesney Martin, 1951–1970

Appointed by President Truman, reappointed by Presidents Eisenhower, Kennedy, Johnson and Nixon. He served almost 20 years. Martin was a former President of the New York Stock Exchange and Assistant Secretary of the Treasury. He had great credentials to become Chairman of the Fed. There are many things to remember him for, but two brief quotes are famous, "It was the Fed's job to lean against the wind" meaning the Fed should counter inflation and unemployment." Also, "the Fed has to take away the punch bowl just when the party gets going!

Arthur Burns, 1970–-1978

Appointed by President Nixon and reappointed by Presidents Ford and Carter Burns was a Columbia University professor and President Eisenhower's economic adviser. He was criticized for excessive pump priming. In 1972 the money supply increased 11 percent and helped Nixon win a landslide re-election.

I had the opportunity to have dinner with Chairman Burns at St. Anselm's College in Manchester, New Hampshire. It was a small group and he was affable and easy-going. I had read about his reputation at the Fed where some of his associates described him as cruel and arrogant. The criticism became more wide spread after he left office. I saw a hint of his impatience and quick temper when a student's question irritated him.

G. William Miller, 1978–1979

Appointed by President Carter, he served just 17 months when Carter appointed him as Secretary of the Treasury. Miller was the former CEO of Textron Corporation in Rhode Island. He didn't have the usual background in finance and economics for the job but was accustomed to running things. At his first meeting of the board he put a sign on the table that said, "Thank you for not smoking." The smokers paid no attention! He also tried to limit long-winded speeches with an egg timer which also was ignored.

Paul Volcker, 1979—1987

Appointed by President Carter and reappointed by President Reagan, Volcker has a background in finance and economics. He served for four years as president of the

New York Fed. I met Chairman Volcker in Boston and he is an imposing figure and speaker.

Alan Greenspan, 1987–2006

An economist appointed by Presidents Reagan and reappointed by Bush 41, Clinton and Bush 43. A famous quote by Alan Greenspan is, "I know you think you understand what you thought I said but I'm not sure you realize that what you heard is not what I meant."

Ben Bernanke, 2006— 2014

Appointed by President Bush and reappointed by President Obama, Ben Bernanke was a tenured professor at Princeton University and chaired the department of economics there. He is now with the Brookings Institute.

Janet Yellen, 2014—

Janet Yellen taught at Harvard and the University of California, Berkley. She served on the Council of Economic Affairs and then became President and CEO of the Federal Reserve of San Francisco. Ms. Yellen then served as Vice Chair of the Federal Reserve Board of Governors. President Obama appointed her as the first female Chair of the Board in 2014.

Alan Greenspan and Ben Bernanke are more well-known than their predecessors and both have received mixed reviews regarding their stewardship of the Fed. There will be much more written in the years ahead.

Most of us assume that the Fed has always enjoyed a high level of independence from any current administration and from other federal agencies, however, the Fed is not immune from political pressure and there have been turf battles between the Fed and Treasury in the past.

William Grieder in his book, "Secrets of the Temple" wrote about such a battle during President Truman's administration.

Countries like Great Britain and France have central banks that work in concert with the elected government. Surprisingly Paul Volcker wrote in his senior thesis at Princeton that the conflicting roles between the Treasury and the Fed should be resolved by combining the Treasury with the Fed. He later revised his proposal.

Volcker"s recommendation was not seriously considered until there was a confrontation between President Truman and Thomas McCabe, Chairman of the Fed. McCabe declared that the Fed would no longer restrain the rise in interest rates. The President forcefully disagreed. Finally the White House announced that the disagreement has been amicably settled and the Fed would keep rates at the current level.

A short time later the Fed said it could not continue with the agreement. President Truman assented to a negotiated settlement between the Treasury and the Fed. In a strange twist, the chief negotiator of the settlement was William McChesney Martin who was Assistant Secretary of the Treasury and soon to be the Fed Chairman. The accord was formally signed in March 1951.

The impact of the accord was rather small in the beginning, however, within two years Martin and other Fed officials began claiming a more sweeping interpretation of the agreement. They claimed it was a declaration of the full independence of the Central Bank.

The scariest month in the financial world began in September 2008 with a cascade of failing financial companies. Henry Paulson, and Ben Bernanke deserve great credit for working together to prevent an all-out collapse of the system.

Lehman Brothers began in 1850 and was one of the oldest and largest investment banks in the country. Lehman filed for bankruptcy on September 10, 2008.

Dick Fuld served for 14 years as the CEO of Lehman. He was the longest serving CEO on Wall Street. Fuld was the driving force in pushing Lehman into increasing volumes of high risk mortgage securities that eventually led to the bankruptcy of his company. It was the largest bankruptcy in US history.

Instead of being "Too Big to Fail" Lehman was described as "Too Big to Save". Paulson thought he had an agreement with Barclays Bank in England but at the last minute Gordon Brown, Prime Minister, and Alastair Darling, Chancellor of the Exchequer squashed the deal.

After Barclays backed out Paulson said there were no other buyers for Lehman. There were no buyers for Merrill Lynch or Bear Stearns either, without substantial government assistance but the word was "let ol Lehman go."

Paulson and Bernanke may have misjudged the reaction to the Lehman bankruptcy. Federal officials had experience with single financial company failures, even very large ones, but the threat of chain reaction was chilling!

After the Lehman demise the Fed made an unprecedented move and opened the Discount Window to investment banks. Equally surprising, the Fed, which previously only excepted AAA securities for collateral on loans, said it would except mortgage-backed securities. The Fed also lowered interest rates. The Lehman failure was earthshaking but immediately ahead was an even more disruptive bankruptcy, AIG.

American International Group, AIG, was the world's largest insurance company with over $1 trillion in assets. Maurice "Hank" Greenberg was the driving force at AIG and was highly regarded in the U.S. and around the world. AIG was one of 30 companies included in the Dow Jones Industrial Average. The company's AAA credit rating was closely guarded by Greenberg.

In 1987 Greenberg and Howard Sosin created the Financial Products Group as part of AIG. Sosin had previously been associated with Michael Milken at Drexel Burnham. When Milken's company blew up Sosin and thirteen of his associates including Joseph Cassano joined him in the FP Group at AIG.

In 1994 Sosin had a falling out with Greenberg and Cassano took over the FP group. Cassano was interested in J.P. Morgan's Bistro computer model that was used to calculate risk in certain investments. Cassano eventually passed on buying it and had his own quants develop a proprietary model.

Cassano claimed his computer model was so good that the odds were 98.5 per cent certain that AIG would never need to make a payment on any credit default swap contracts they wrote or collateral debt obligations they were insuring.

A credit default swap (CDS) is a derivative contract that acts as a form of insurance on a bond, loan or CDO.

A collateralized debt obligation (CDO) is a security backed by a pool of other debt securities, i.e. mortgages, auto loans, credit card loans, etc. A CDO was typically sliced into tranches and sold to investors.

It's not surprising perhaps that the FP group operated like a giant hedge fund. FP sold CDS's on billions of dollars of CDOs to just about every bank and Wall Street firm. A significant volume of the contracts FP wrote were backed by subprime mortgages that began losing value. From a handful of people the FP group had grown to a highly profitable part of AIG which contributed 17.5 percent of the company's profit in 2005. By the end of 2007 AIG had sold CDS's on various securities worth $440 billion.

AIG was an extreme example of interconnectedness, so much so there was concern if AIG failed it would bring down Goldman Sachs and Morgan Stanley.

I wrote earlier about the Commodities Futures Trading Commission and how Robert Rubin and Larry Summers threatened Brooksley Born with legislation if she continued her efforts to have her agency regulate CDS's. Also, how Senator Graham included the Enron loophole and legislation.

Unfortunately it left the FP group virtually free from regulation. AIG, the insurance part of the business, began to run into problems with the SEC in 2003 and paid two hefty fines for helping clients engaged in improper accounting.

In 2005 Elliot Spitzer, the Attorney General of New York, joined in accusing Greenberg of "sham transactions". Greenberg said they were minor foot faults but eventually paid a fine of $15 million without admitting any guilt. Greenberg was forced out of the company he built into a world-class company. He was succeeded by Martin Sullivan, a long time AIG insurance guy. Sullivan had the approval of Spitzer but not the whole-hearted endorsement of Greenberg.

One might assume that Sullivan would view the derivative world with some caution, however, Sullivan immediately let Cassano double FPs exposure to subprime mortgage-backed CDOs. By September 2008 AIG had 2.7 trillion swap contracts with over 2000 counter parties.

In 2008 Price Waterhouse Coopers, AIG's auditor, questioned the value of swaps on the company's books. The audit committee was chaired by Michael Sutton who was the former chief accountant for the SEC. He brought his committee's concerns to the full board.

Sullivan expressed confidence in the values on the books but did finally agree with the outside auditors. In early 2008 AIG recorded a $5.3 billion loss for the previous quarter. When the loss became public AIG's stock lost 20 percent of its value in two days.

Quick action was needed before TARP was passed, but AIG did not come under the jurisdiction of the Fed. Several writers have taken the position that the Fed did not have the authority to rescue Lehman Brothers, however, that's exactly what the Fed did to rescue AIG.

Cassano was fired but he kept his $34 million bonus from the previous year and inexplicably he was given a rich consulting contract. Cassano, who had major responsibility for AIG's impending failure was dubbed "the man who crashed the world."

Paulson and Bernanke described AIG as systemically important and had to be saved not just for the financial community but for the entire economy.

After the government saved AIG and it was clear AIG would honor its commitments, Warren Buffet invested $5 billion in Goldman Sachs in exchange for preferred shares that paid a 10 percent dividend as well as the right to purchase common shares at a discount. It was a good deal for Buffet, but his confidence resulted in another $5 billion shares sold the next day.

John Mack at Morgan Stanley had been negotiating with the Japanese bank Mitsubishi for a $9 billion investment. Mack was getting desperate because the price of Morgan Stanley stock kept dropping. The deal was closed after AIG was bailed out.

Bernanke said the Fed had reached it's limit after the $85 billion investment in AIG and he kept urging Paulson to go to Congress for legislation for substantial funds for additional bailouts. Sheila Bair was panicking that the FDIC could run out of funds… the insurance fund was down to $30 billion and she asked Paulson to include an increase in the FDIC credit line at the Treasury from the current $45 billion amount. Paulson went ahead with his TARP proposal but did not include Bair's request.

Chapter 35

Fannie And Freddie: Signs Of Trouble

John Taylor, Professor of Economics at Stanford University, wrote about the early warning signs of troubles in the financial markets. Professor Taylor wrote, "signs of severe trouble flared on Thursday, August 9, 2007, when traders in New York, London and other financial centers around the world faced a dramatic and sudden change in conditions in the money markets."

"Interest rates on medium-term inter-bank loans measured in LIBOR* surged, compared with the interest rates on overnight inter-bank loans."[1]

Interest rates on trillions of dollars of loans and securities are linked to LIBOR.

The lending between banks in the LIBOR market is unsecured and it appeared that rising delinquencies and losses in US mortgage loans was causing increasing concern in the international markets.

After a long period of calm we were heading into a period of uncertainty and eventual turmoil, because of the questions about the underlying quality of U.S. mortgages and mortgage securities.

The housing bubble had reached an unbelievable size by the middle of 2007 but it was not just the size of the bubble that caused it to collapse, it was the composition. An interesting fact is the level of defaults and foreclosures were far worse in the United States then in other countries which were experiencing financial trouble.

Subprime loans were rare or nonexistent outside the U.S. NINJA

---

* LIBOR stands for the London Inter-Bank Offered Rate

loans, meaning no income, no job, no assets, and ALt-A loans were available only in this country. ALt-A loans were nonconforming loans, best described as not quite prime and not quite subprime. ALt-A loans are of special interest because as Roger Lowenstein observed, "they made a relatively small part of Fannie's portfolio but represented fully one half of the losses."[2]

In 2007, about a year before the government takeover of Fannie and Freddie in September, 2008, Fannie had capital of $44 billion and Freddie $27 billion. It was a tiny amount of capital in both companies to support a combined $5 trillion business.

Although the two companies operated for many years with separate boards of directors, huge and expensive executive staff and magnificent headquarters, Fannie and Freddie were in the same business.

The following is a condensed balance sheet of the two companies at the time of the takeover.

	Fannie Mae		Freddie Mac
Mortgages (Billions)	$484	debt	$1535
Mortgage Backed Securities	1,1037	other	71
Other Assets	157	equity	71
	$ 1,678		$ 1,678

The combined balance sheet of the two companies was huge at $1.678 trillion, but like Citigroup both Fannie and Freddie had enormous off-balance sheet obligations from guaranteeing mortgages. Fannie had $2.118 trillion and Freddie $1.381 trillion.

The implied government guarantees became actual government obligations with the takeovers.

Combined F & F Balance Sheets	$ 1.678 trillion
Off Balance Sheet Fannie	2.118 trillion
Off Balance Sheet Freddie	1.381 trillion
	$ 5.177 trillion

Fannie and Freddie represented a $5 trillion business which is now owned by the American taxpayers.

Roger Lowenstein wrote, "Fannie's and Freddie's core capital was approximately 2.5 percent and under 0.5 percent for mortgage backed securities, Fannie's leverage was as high as 100 to 1 and Freddie's 170 to 1. By comparison Lehman and Bear were pikers."[3]

After a long period of calm house prices began falling dramatically and the financial markets were heading into great uncertainty and turmoil as the value of mortgage loans and securities became a panic.

The housing bubble finally burst in part because of its gigantic size but more importantly because of the size of a toxic mix of mortgage products. It would not have happened without the total involvement of the US Government in promoting and underwriting the volume of subprime mortgages and securities.

The Housing and Economic Recovery Act, 2008, was passed with bipartisan support in Congress and signed by President Bush on July 30, 2008. Henry Paulson, Secretarty of the Treasury, had made a commitment to solve the Fannie and Freddie problem before he left office after the November election.

Paulson hired Ruth Porat and Robert Scully from Morgan Stanley to recommend a solution, (hiring Goldman Sachs, his alma mater, would've been a conflict.) Porat and Scully came up with three options: One, Fannie and Freddie could raise more capital. It was not a viable option, both companies stock price was in single digits and earlier attempts to raise additional capital were not successful. Two: a receivership and liquidation, which would be very difficult and a long time frame. It would also be destructive to a functioning housing market. Three: A conservatorship, which Paulson accepted, with a government take-over of both Fannie and Freddie.

The Act replaced OFHEO with a new federal agency, the Federal Housing Finance Agency, FHFA, to regulate both companies. James B. Lockhart III became the head of FHFA with greatly expanded authority.

The law gave the Treasury virtually unlimited authority to advance funds to Fannie and Freddie. The Federal Reserve Bank of New York was given authority to lend funds as needed.

Lockhart, with Paulson's help, immediately dismissed Daniel Mudd, CEO of Fannie, and Richard Syron, CEO of Freddie, and removed all the directors of both companies.

The Treasury announced that $100 billion was available for each company. Also little noticed, Paulson said the Fed would buy $500 billion of Fannie's and Freddie's mortgage-backed securities.

President Obama appointed Tim Geithner to succeed Paulson as

Secretary of the Treasury. Geithner apparently forgot the commitment for complete transparency and quietly removed the bail-out caps for Fannie and Freddie on Christmas Eve of 2009.

Lockhart reassured the markets lenders that Fannie and Freddie would continue to have funds to purchase conforming loans and grow their portfolios without limit.

Chapter 36

The SEC Sues Fannie And Freddie

In December 2011, the Securities and Exchange Commission filed a lawsuit against three former executives of Fannie Mae for "making a series of materially false and misleading public disclosures... concerning the company's exposure to subprime and ALt-A loans."

The executives Daniel Mudd, Chief Executive Officer, Enrico Delavecchia, Chief Risk Officer and Thomas Lund, Executive Vice President, were charged with violation of the anti-fraud and reporting provisions of securities laws.

A similar lawsuit was filed against Richard Syron at Freddie Mac, Chief Executive Officer, also Patricia Cook, Executive Vice President, and Daniel Besenuis, Senior Vice President.

Peter Wallison wrote about the lawsuits in the Wall Street Journal, "For the first time in a government report, the complaint has made it clear that the two GSEs played a major role in creating the demand for low quality mortgages before the 2008 financial crisis. More importantly the SEC is saying that Fannie and Freddie, the largest buyers and securitizers of subprime and other low quality mortgages, hid the size of their purchases from the market."

"Through these acts of securities fraud, they did not just mislead investors, they deprived analysts, risk managers, rating agencies and even financial regulators of vital data about market risks that could have prevented this crisis."[1]

Because Fannie and Freddie were the dominant players in the home mortgage market, the deliberate under-reporting of the volume of high-risk funds, led others involved in the market to assume if the giants had zero or minimal exposure as Mudd and Syron repeatedly claimed, then the overall volume of subprime loans had to be relatively small. It was a bad assumption.

The SEC alleges that Fannie's second-quarter 2008 report, issued just a month before the takeover, that its ALt-A loans accounted for only $306 billion of its guarantee exposure, the real number was $647 billion.

August 20, 2008, Mudd said in a radio broadcast, "Fannie had zero percent exposure to subprime loans."

Syron said at a UBS conference on May 14, 2007, "As we discussed in the past, at the end of 2006, Freddie had basically no subprime exposure." Later on December 11, 2007, at Goldman Sachs Conference Syron said, "In terms of our insight into the subprime stuff, we didn't buy any subprime loans."

Fannie and Freddie both had special loan programs that internally were considered sub-prime but had positive-sounding labels and were not reported accurately as subprime loans.

Fannie had at least two such programs. One was known as "Alternative Qualifying Mortgages" and the other "Expanded Approval Mortgages." Both programs included eliminating or reducing traditional underwriting requirements. In 2007, four instance, Fannie reported $8.3 billion in EA Loans. The real number was $94 billion.

Freddie had a special program known as "Touch More Loans" which also included reduced requirements. Another program was called "Home Possible" which allowed lower down payments and other exceptions that made such loans subprime.

I wrote previously about the compensation scandals at both GSEs which destroyed so much of the credibility both companies had enjoyed, but the SEC lawsuits, which still have not been brought to trial in 2013, run to over 50 pages, further documenting the corruption at both Fannie and Freddie.

Many politicians want you to think Fannie and Freddie are old news and you will not care about what really happened. The GSEs were essentially one company, one of the largest corporations in the world which was destroyed by politics.

Chapter 37

Financial Crisis Inquiry Commission

I wrote earlier that initial reports on major events are often changed over time when additional information becomes available, however sometimes later reports are so partisan in assigning responsibility for things that went wrong they are unreliable.

I believe the Financial Crisis Inquiry Commission Report which was sent to President Obama in May, 2009 and released in January 2011, which should have been the definitive analysis of the causes of the crisis was flawed because of political bias.

The Commission was created by an act of Congress after 18 months of work at great expense to the taxpayers, a 900-page double-spaced report was submitted to the Congress and the President.

The Commission was made up of six Democrats and four Republicans. Phil Angelides was appointed Chairman by Harry Reed and Nancy Pelosi. The other Democratic members were Brooksley Born, Byron Gegiou, Bob Gramm, Heather Murren, and John Thomson.

Bill Thomas was appointed Vice Chairman by Mitch McConnell and John Boehner. The other Republicans were Keith Hennesey, Douglas Holtz-Eakin and Peter Wallison.

All six Democrats signed the final report. Three Republicans, Keith Hennessey Douglas Holtz-Eakin and Bill Thomas, signed a dissenter report and Peter Wallison wrote a 100-page detailed dissenting report.

Although few of us have any interest in the FCIC report it is important because legislators have used the majority report in supporting new laws and regulations. The Dodd-Frank Act for instance has left open over 200 rules for such things as margin requirements, swaps and futures. The rules were not published by late 2012, still waiting for input from legislators and regulators.

It's not unusual for members of a federal commission to have different views and opinions about the subject matter. It is unusual and unfair for the minority members to be excluded from scheduled meetings with individuals who are called to testify and to have secret meetings. Any dissenting opinions were excluded from the final report.

The majority report did not assign any responsibility for the financial crisis to the Clinton or Bush administrations nor were any members of Congress held accountable for their role in the Fannie and Freddie failures. Andrew Cuomo, who initiated HUD goals and even threatened to fine the two companies $10,000 per day for failure to meet the goals, wasn't even asked to appear before the Commission.

It may be harsh to say anyone would play politics with an economic disaster like the financial crisis, however if one looks at the way Angelides, the Chairman, ran the Commission, it's apparent his personal bias prevented any hope of a bipartisan reliable report.

Angelides was an early supporter of Michael Dukakis in California which led to his chairing the Democratic Party in California from 1991 to 1993. He went on to serve as Treasurer of California from 1998- 2007.

Angelides developed a close relationship with the Greenlining Institute, a militant housing rights group, located in San Francisco. He often spoke about "the gap between rich and poor" and the need for more financial resources for the "under-served." He believed CRA was the vehicle to close the gap.

Paul Sperry wrote "Angelides... steered billions of dollars in state funds to CRA friendly banks that loaded up on subprime and other risky mortgages. Beginning in 1999, he sank billions more into subprime securities backed by Freddie Mac and he did not let up until he left office in 2007."

The Greenlining Institute advised Angelides where to invest state funds in banks that received good CRA ratings. In an interview with the American Banker Anjelides said, "It helps us spot banks that are great players in community reinvestment. It helps us make judgments about where to put our resources."[1]

The following statement from the FCIC Report is a major reason the Republican members of the Commission filed dissenting reports

The FCIC statement: "the GSEs contributed to, but were not a primary cause of the Financial Crisis... They followed rather than led, the Wall Street Firms"... The Community Reinvestment Act (CRA) was not a significant factor in subprime lending."

I wrote at length about CRA earlier, but the following quote by Jamie Gorelick speaking to a group of bankers when she was vice-chairman of Fannie in 2000, illustrates how important CRA really was. "Since 1997, you (bankers) have done nearly $7 billion in CRA business, but it is just the beginning... Fannie Mae is committed to over $20 billion in targeted CRA business."

Before quoting from Peter Wallison's lengthy dissenting report let me give two definitions of abbreviation he uses, NTM refers to nontraditional mortgages, which means mortgages that were not prime loans. PMBS, refers to private mortgage-backed securities backed by subprime loans or other NTMs.

Wallison wrote, "one of the many myths about the financial crisis is that Wall Street banks led the way into subprime lending and the GSEs followed. The Commission majorities report adopts this idea as a way of explaining why Fannie and Freddie acquired so many NTMs. This simply does not align with the facts. Not only were Wall Street institutions small factors in the subprime PMBS market, but well before 2002, Fannie and Freddie were much bigger players in the entire PMBS market in the business of acquiring NTM and other subprime loans. Fannie and Freddie had already acquired at least $701 billion by 2001. Obviously the GSEs did not have to follow anyone before 2002. In 2002 when the entire PMBS market was $134 billion Fannie and Freddie acquired $206 billion in whole subprime mortgages and $368 billion in other NTMs demonstrating again the GSEs were no strangers to risk lending well before the PMBS market began to develop."[2]

Wallison wrote in detail about the material supplied to the Commission by Edward Pinto, the former Chief Credit Officer at Fannie. Pinto provided a 70 page fully sourced memorandum concerning the level of subprime and other high-risk mortgages before the crisis. He documented the effort by HUD over two decades and two administrations to increase home ownership by reducing traditional mortgage writing standards.

Pinto's work was not made available to the Commission members nor was Pinto asked to meet with the Commission.

Chapter 38

Fannie And Freddie Timeline

1938. Fannie Mae is established as a government agency to support the housing industry during the Great Depression. It was a major development in President Roosevelt's administration.

1968. President Johnson wants to remove both GSE's from his budget and legislation is passed to make both Fannie and Freddie public /private corporations.

The legislation provided for Freddie Mac to be established in 1970. Freddy's role is primarily to bail out struggling savings and loans.

The government guarantee of the obligations of both companies was changed to an "implied guarantee."

1968. The Fair Housing Act of 1968 is also known as Title VIII of the Civil Rights Act October 1968. The law prohibits discrimination in the role of rental, and financing of dwellings. It also is known as the anti-redlining act.

The Community Reinvestment Act, CRA, was passed and signed into law in 1977 by President Jimmy Carter. It was designed to "encourage" bankers to meet the needs of borrowers in all segments of the community where they did business.

The Federal Reserve Bank of Boston under the leadership of Richard Syron, publishes a mortgage study which alleges pervasive discrimination in mortgage lending by area bankers. The methodology is critically flawed, however, the Clinton administration and bank regulators adopt the study without question.

The Federal Housing Enterprises Financial Safety and Soundness Act is passed in 1992, it is generally known as the GSE Act.

Henry Gonzales, Texas Democrat and Chairman of the House Banking Committee, sponsored the legislation with extensive input from ACORN.

The bill had been in the works for a long period of time and had many provisions, however the stated purpose was to protect the American taxpayers from another bailout like the S&L bailout.

Unfortunately the GSE Act did just the opposite; for the first time in our history HUD was given authority to set affordable housing goals for Fannie and Freddie to buy nontraditional mortgages with reduced underwriting standards.

Initially the law specified that 30% of mortgages purchased should be for low- moderate income families. The trend towards increasingly risky mortgages had begun.

1992. Bill Clinton is elected President and members of his administration embrace the Boston Fed Study. Attorney General Janet Reno prosecutes bankers and threatens others under the Fair Housing Act and CRA.

1995. President Clinton approves new CRA regulations that mandate bankers to use "innovative" or "flexible" "underwriting practices. He issues executive orders to greatly strengthened CRA practices, including making CRA ratings public.

1995. HUD authorizes Fannie and Freddie to purchase subprime mortgage loans.

1995. Henry Cisneros, HUD Secretary, announces that 42% of each GSEs purchases of mortgage loans should go to families with low-moderate income.

1997. Freddie and Bear Stearns securitize the first public offering uf CRA loans guaranteed by Freddie.

1997. Fannie launches it's CRA initiative to finance $1 billion CRA loans by years end.

Fannie announces a program to buy 3% down payment loans.

2000. Andrew Cuomo, HUD Secretary endorses the Boston Fed Study and uses his authority to substantially ramp-up affordable housing goals Fannie and Freddie for the. 2001- 2003.

Cuomo's following goals were:

1. Low Moderate Income Goal. At least 50% of each GSE's purchases should be for families with incomes no greater than the area median income. (It's an increase from 42% to 50%.)

2. For every mortgage acquired that did not qualify as a low-moderate income loan, Fannie or Freddie had to acquire a nonconforming loan.

3. Special Affordable Goal. At least 20% of each GSE's purchases should be for very low income families.

4. Underserved Goal. At least 30% of each GSE's purchases should be for underserved areas.

2000. Vice chair Jamie Gorelick, of Fannie, said at an American Bankers meeting on October 30, 2000 "Since 1977, we have done nearly $7 billion in specialty targeted CRA business with you bankers, but before the decade is over, Fannie Mae is committed to finance over $20 billion in specialty targeted CRA business and over 500 million billion altogether."

"Some people have assumed we don't buy tough loans. Let me correct the misinformation right now. We want your CRA loans because they help us meet our housing goals."

According to the Clinton Foundation Center for Community Change, between 1993-2000, loans mandated by CRA totaled $800 billion.

Jamie Gorelick was appointed by President Clinton to the Fannie Mae board in 1998 as vice chairman. She served until 2003 and her compensation was $26 million.

2001. Franklin Raines, CEO Fannie, announces the "The American Dream Commitment" a ten-year $2 trillion dollar pledge for underserved communities. Raines served for 10 years, his total compensation was $90 million.

2000. George W. Bush is elected President and follows a curious dual path of following the Clinton housing agenda but also urging Congress to rein in Fannie and Freddie as threats to the economy.

2000. President Bush, soon after being elected, is urged by several holdover President Clinton housing activists to increase affordable housing goals from 50% to 57%. Bush agrees to an increase to 56% over four years.

2001. John Snow, Secretary of the Treasury, urges Congress with Bush's support to pass legislation to transfer supervisory and regulatory responsibility to the Treasury. The legislation isn't passed.

2003. Bush supports the "American Dream Down Payment Act" which subsidizes down payment and closing costs.

2004. He enlists his Secretary of HUD, Mel Martinez, to help 5.5 million additional minorities own their own homes.

2004. Fannie and Freddie purchase $175 billion subprime mortgage securities and from 2005 through 2006 they purchase approximately $1 trillion subprime and ALt-A loans.

2006. The Bush Administration strikes a deal with Fannie and Freddie to limit the size of their investment portfolios, however Fannie still bought $180 billion for the year.

2006. Daniel Mudd, CEO Fannie, and Richard Syron, CEO Freddie assuring their shareholders and the public their exposure to subprime and ALt-A loans is immaterial, later disclosure show both companies were deliberately disguising substantial exposures to high-risk investments.

Fannie and Freddie are losing money at an alarming rate and appear headed for insolvency. Attempts to raise new capital are marginally successful at Fannie but not Freddie. Hank Paulson, Secretary of the Treasury, is committed to solving the problem before leaving office.

2008.The Housing and Economic Recovery Act is passed and signed into law by George Bush on July 30, 2008. The law replaced OFHEO with a new federal agency, The Federal Housing Finance Agency to regulate Fannie and Freddie.

The law gives the Treasury virtually unlimited authority to advance funds as necessary to GSE's. The Federal Reserve Bank of New York is given specific authority to provide the funds..

2008. In September Director Lockhart, FHFA head, dismisses Daniel Mudd, CEO Fannie and Richard Syron, CEO Freddie, and also removes all of the directors of both companies. There is some debate over whether both GSE's are insolvent because their balance sheets show assets in excess of liabilities, however the off-balance-sheet obligations clearly show the companies are insolvent.

The Treasury makes $200 billion available to each GSE for recapitalization, however it is often overlooked that the New York Fed agreed to buy $500 billion of Fannie and Freddie's mortgage-backed securities.

Christmas Eve, Timothy Geithner, the new Secretary of the Treasury quietly removes the $400 billion bailout limit on both GSE's.

The Securities and Exchange Commission files a lawsuit on December10.

2011. against three former executives at Freddie Mac: Richard Syron, CEO, Patricia Cook, Executive Vice Presidenand Donald Bisenuis, Senior Vice President, "for a series of materially false and misleading public disclosures."

A similar lawsuit was filed on December 16, 2011, against three former Fannie Mae executives: Daniel Mudd, CEO, Enrico Delavecchia, Chief Risk Officer, and Thomas Lund, Executive Vice President.

Peter Wallison wrote in the Wall Street Journal on December 21, 2011, "through these alleged acts of securities fraud they did not just mislead investors, they deprived analysts, risk managers, rating agencies and even financial regulators of vital data about market risks that could have prevented the crisis."

Wallison also reported that he did not turn up any analyst that came close to estimating the actual number of subprime and other low quality mortgages.

The under reporting of high risk loans led people involved in the market to believe if the two giants, Fannie and Freddie, had minimal exposure to subprime and subprime like loans, then the outstanding volume of such loans had to be relatively low. The blatant dishonesty by the leadership of both companies about their exposure caused that assumption to be very wrong.

Chapter 39

The Nationalization Of American Banks

The Troubled Asset Relief Program, TARP, sometimes called The Toxic Asset Relief Program was originally presented to Congress on a three page $700 billion program to buy troubled assets from the banks. Henry Paulson had not done a good job of convincing members of Congress and the public that his plan was needed not just to save Wall Street but also Main Street. Speaker Pelosi, in a partisan response to his plan, rejected it and blamed George Bush and his free-market principles for our problems.

A major problem with the Paulson plan was it was impossible for the government to decide in a tight time frame what assets to buy and at what prices. On September 30, 2008, the house defeated the measure by 228 to 205.

There was enormous pressure on George Bush and the Congress to get something done. Bernanke continued to press Paulson to change his plan from buying assets to injecting capital in the banks in exchange for preferred shares. The shares would carry a 5 percent dividend which would increase to 9 percent after five years. The government also would get warrants to buy common shares at depressed prices.

Congress passed TARP and President Bush signed it. The government nationalized the banking system with a three page bill.

On Sunday, October 13, 2008 Paulson called the CEOs of nine of the largest financial institutions and told them to be at his office in the Treasury building the next day at 3 PM he told each that Ben Bernanke and Sheila Bair would be at the meeting but did not provide any details.

Richard Kocavick, CEO of Wells Fargo, said he would not attend, but changed his mind. Paulson, known for his forceful manner, got quickly to the point. He emphasized no changes would be accepted and it was an offer no one could refuse to accept.

The following is a list of the CEOs in attendance and the amounts each company would receive:

	BILLION
Vikran Pandit, Citigroup	25
Jamie Dimon, J.P. Morgan	25
Richard Kocavick, Wells Fargo	25
Ken Lewis, Bank of America	15
John Thain, Merrill Lynch	10
Lloyd Blankfein, Goldman Sachs	10
John Mack, Morgan Stanley	10
Robert Kelly, Bank New York Mellon	3
Ronald Logue, State Street Bank	2
	$125 Billion

Bank of America had not completed the deal to acquire Merrill Lynch; the $10 billion for Merrill would be added to the Bank America total after the acquisition.

Citigroup came back in November for another $20 billion plus guarantees for a $300 billion pool of securities and loans of unknown value. It's interesting to note that only two of the CEOs listed, Blankfein and Dimon, are still at their companies four years later.

Although the regulations regarding capital may have changed after TARP, at the time only Citigroup and Merrill Lynch were insolvent. Bank of America was a little shaky, Kocavick at Wells Fargo didn't want the funds and complained he took Wachovia off their hands and didn't ask for government help. Jamie Dimon happily accepted the funds but didn't need it. None of the others were really a threat to the economy.

The program allocated another $125 billion for banks across the country. John Allison, CEO of BB&T Bank, said he lobbied against the bailout bill. He represented one of the largest and best run banks in the country, but both Henry Paulson and Ben Bernanke refused to talk with him about the pending legislation.

Allison said he received a call from the regulators after the bill passed.

They agreed his bank had sufficient capital, more than required, and was profitable. However, they warned him about new capital requirements that were being considered. He was told they were prepared to send in a team to re-examine his bank's capital position if he refused TARP funds.[1]

Allison agreed to accept the allocated funds. After the new capital rules were applied BB&T remained more than well capitalized.

Although the government was heavy-handed in dealing with some of the bankers that balked at taking TARP funds, Paulson and Bernanke had a legitimate concern about having two bank lists, Bad Banks and Good Banks. Paulson's and Bernanke's emissaries could have handled it better.

After Congress passed the TARP bill the government took the position it would not release the names of the banks or the the amounts they received to the public. The backlash from members of Congress and the media was fierce. There were threats of audits and new regulations until the government backed down. The power and sometimes arrogance of our government should not be under estimated.

Thousands of banks failed during the depression, many were sound enough, but could not weather a full-scale bank run. Thomas Sowell pointed out that, "90 percent of the failing banks were in small communities and almost all were in states with laws against branch banking."

"Canada had ten banks with 3,000 branches across the country and did not have one bank failure despite the fact they experienced the same depression. The Canadian government did not provide deposit insurance."[2]

The record in this country had been very good for seventy years and then everything changed in mid July, 2008. IndyMac Bank faced an old-fashioned bank run. IndyMac was the short name for Independent Mortgage Corporation. The bank was spun off from Angelo Mozillo's Countrywide Mortgage, not surprisingly it specialized in subprime and ALt-A mortgages. It was a relatively small bank but had $18 billion in uninsured deposits.

Problems at IndyMac were well-known, finally the Office of Thrift Supervision issued a downgrade in June 2008, John Reich, head of the OTS and Sheila Baer, FDIC, both received letters from Sen. Chuck Schumer stating, "I am concerned that IndyMac's financial deterioration poses significant risk to both taxpayers and borrowers and that the bank could face a failure if proscriptive measures are not taken."[3]

Sheila Bair wrote, "The impetus for that provocative letter and Senator's Schumer's decision to make it public remain a mystery."

Bair was being generous, the senator should not have made such a letter public. The media pounced on the story and the TV cameras showed long lines of customers lining up to withdraw their funds. Some customers waited days to receive their funds and there were many sad human interest stories. Bair received much deserved criticism for not responding more quickly and positively. Uncertainty fuels a panic.

James Barth, professor at Auburn University, publicly faulted the FDIC for not doing an adequate job of explaining the role of the FDIC to the "every day American."

Bair initiated a public relations campaign to explain the FDIC's role in a bank failure, however, she had good reason to criticize the media for not reporting information accurately which added to the panic. Bair's agency was hit with the largest bailout expense ever. The cost was a whopping $10.7 billion.

She vowed any other bank failure would be handled more decisively. The opportunity was just around the corner. Washington Mutual the famous WaMu (pronounced way moo) was on the verge of insolvency in September.

Wa Mu was the sixth largest bank in the country and the largest Thrift with $300 billion in assets. As was described in a previous chapter, it was a reckless operation that should have been subject to cease and desist orders much earlier.

David Bonderman of Texas Pacific Group, TPG, was one of the savviest and most successful private equity investors in the US. He was a friend of Kerry Killinger the CEO of WaMu and had invested heavily in the savings and loan.

There has been frequent misreporting of his investment and ultimate loss in WaMu. In April, 2008, he headed a group of people that invested $7 billion in WaMu. His personal share was $1.35 billion of that amount. In six months the value of their investments had lost most of it's value.

In early 2008, WaMu's problems were increasing by the day. An unfortunate part of the story is that John Reich, head of OTS, and Sheila Bair were at war with each other and there was little cooperation between them. On September 11, one of the largest commercial customers withdrew its account. Withdrawals accelerated too well over $1 billion per day.

Bonderman, was part of the discussion to provide additional funds, however, no agreement was reached. When WaMu failed Bonderman and TPG investors lost all of their investment.

Finally on September 25, 2008, the OTS closed WaMu. Chase bought the assets and all the deposits, insured and uninsured for $1.8 billion. The holding company filed for bankruptcy after the failure of WaMu and the shareholders and bondholders lost their investment.

Bair was pleased with the "seamless transition" and very happy it didn't cost her agency anything. However, the inevitable questions were raised. Was there a better way to minimize the losses to the shareholders and debt holders?

John Allison raised some serious criticisms of the FDIC's handling of the Washington Mutual failure. He in fact said, "unquestionably, the handling of WaMu forced the failure of Wachovia."

Allison referred to the IndyMac problem and the legitimate concern the regulators had if a similar situation occurred at WaMu. However, he said the manner in which they chose to handle WaMu was even more destructive. They decided to take the extra losses created by covering the uninsured depositors from WaMu's bondholders. The bondholders had expected significant losses on their bonds, but the losses were more than they had expected because the FDIC had taken part of the money that should have been available to pay bondholders and given it to uninsured depositors. This is a complete contradiction to past practice. The bondholders suddenly realized that there is no rule of law when government regulators are involved "...." once the bond market saw how Wa Mu's creditors had been treated, the market closed for Wachovia."[4]

Whether you agree with Mr. Allison or not it's an inescapable fact that uncertainty has a destructive effect in the financial markets.

Wachovia was the fourth largest bank holding company and bank in the US. The bank had a national charter and was regulated by the Fed and OCC. Ken Thompson, the CEO, was well known as an aggressive dealmaker and risk taker. The record was clear that Wachovia was headed for insolvency well before it's collapse.

Thompson's reputation was damaged several years earlier when Wachovia paid a large fine for being involved in a major money laundering game with Mexican drug lords.

In 1998 he acquired the Money Store, a company that specialized in home equity loans and subprime mortgages. Thompson paid $2.1 billion for the Money Store and sold it two years later for loss of $1.7 billion.

In 2006 he acquired the Golden West Savings and Loan from Herbert and Marion Sandler. The Sandlers had purchased the S and L in 1963 for

$3.8 million and in the next 30 years they built the sleepy little bank into a powerhouse with over 250 branches. By 2006 they had written more than $100 billion adjustable rate mortgages (ARMs). The ARMs evolved into Pick A Pay mortgages.

There were all kinds of ARMs but Pick A Pay were the most toxic mortgages invented. Borrowers were allowed to make monthly payments that were less than the stated interest. Deficiencies were added to the balance of the loan, all of which was subject to resets at maturity.

George McCarthy, a housing economist at the Ford Foundation said, "The option ARM is like a neutron bomb. It's going to kill all the people but leave the house still standing." The surprising thing is the Sandler's didn't sell the loans, they were kept in portfolio.

Lehman Brothers representatives approached Ken Thompson about buying Golden West. Apparently without much due diligence, Thompson agreed to buy Golden West for $26 billion. He later said, "this will either cement my reputation or get me fired." The Sandler's sold at the top of the market and Thompson was fired two years later.

Tim Geithner, at the New York Fed, and John Dugan, OCC, began pressing Sheila Bair at the FDIC for an assisted takeover of Wachovia by Citigroup. The law requires that the FDIC find the least cost resolution in any take over. Wachovia was literally hours away from failure and Bair was extremely angry that she had been excluded from any deliberations about Wachovia until the last minute.

The New York Fed and the OCC were responsible for the near failure of the fourth largest bank in the country. The plan to merge Wachovia with Citi, the largest financial company at the time, and the worst financial company, didn't make sense to Sheila Bair and more importantly didn't make sense to the American taxpayers. Fortunately, Wells Fargo and Richard Kovacevich stepped in at the last minute and purchased Wachovia without government assistance.

Chapter 40

The Death Star

The federal bank examiners acknowledged long after Citi was in trouble they had never heard of structured investment vehicles,(SIVs), until July 2006. The admission was in spite of the fact Citi had sold seven different funds with a total value of $80 billion. It certainly wasn't secret. Later the federal examiners began referring to Citi as the "Death Star".

Citi's problems were well-known. In September, 2004, the Japanese banking authorities ordered Citi to close it's extensive private banking operation because of serious violations of Japanese laws. It was a major black eye.

The New York Fed ordered Citi to improve its compliance and oversight responsibilities before it would allow Citi to make any more acquisitions. It was not just a letter, it was an order, and impacted Citi's ongoing program of acquisitions that influenced it stock price.

The Fed also cut Citi's rating on risk management from satisfactory to fair. In spite of the Fed's formal warnings, Citi continued to expand its high-risk mortgage business and off-balance-sheet assets.

Although Citi had ignored the Feds warning the ban was lifted in 2006. William Rutledge, head of supervision at the New York Fed, said "Citi had made significant progress in improving its compliance and risk management." The huge bailout of Citi was less than two years down the road. Mr. Rutledge could not have been more wrong.

Sheila Bair wrote in her book, "Bull by the Horns," I frequently wonder whether if Citi had not been in trouble, would we have had those massive bailout programs? So many decisions were made through the prism of that one institutions needs."[1]

It's a question we can't answer, but it is a fact that Citi received special treatment from the New York Fed and the Comptroller of the Currency. Citi was given a forbearance agreement by the Fed and the Department of Justice to violate the Glass-Steagall Act which has been on the books since 1933.

In the 1970s the legendary Walter Wriston acquired a management consulting firm. The Fed ordered him to get rid of it because it wasn't a business incident to banking. A very angry Wriston tried unsuccessfully to argue that banking by its very nature is a consulting business.

The Glass—Steagall Act was challenged over the years, but a major breakthrough happened in 1996. The Fed interpreted section 20 of the Act to allow banks to derive 25 percent of their revenue from investments incident to banking. The OCC began taking a very liberal definition of the term "incident to banking."

In 2003, the Federal Accounting Standards Board, (FASB) issued a new ruling which allowed such investments as collateralized debt obligations, (CDOs) and structured investment vehicles (SIVs) to be moved off the banks balance sheet to a largely undisclosed balance sheet. A CDO is a security backed by a pool of other securities like mortgages and consumer loans.

Technically Citi could keep it's huge volume of SIV's off it's balance sheet because it's customers owned the SIV. There was an important feature, however, that would blow up and cause major losses.

Citi could estimate losses as long as there wasn't a trigger that changed the ownership of the investments. When the markets began to tank Citi investors wanted out of the funds, and Citi had to write down the assets when they were brought back on to the balance sheet.

Bair criticized John Dugan, the Comptroller of the Currency, when she said, "Citi bank N.A. became the dumping ground for Citigroup's toxic assets."[2]

It's hard to accept the many senior banking officials had so little knowledge of Cit's off-balance-sheet assets. In the period of 2007-2008, Citi had $1.8 trillion in assets on its balance sheet and $2 trillion on it's off-balance-sheet.

A terrible example of the lack of oversight and supervision by the Fed and the OCC was that Citi was allowed to continue paying dividends in 2007 and into 2008, in spite of continuing large losses.

Citi reported losses in the fourth quarter of 2007 of $9.8 billion. The loss in the first quarter 2008 was $5.1 billion, second quarter loss $2.5 billion, third quarter loss $2.8 billion and fourth quarter loss $8.29 billion. The total loss for five consecutive quarters was $28.5 billion.

Citi paid $10.7 billion in dividends in 2007 and $3.5 billion in 2008. Any other bank, especially a smaller less connected bank, would have been issued a cease and desist order much earlier.

Sheila Bair was treated with respect in meetings with Paulson and Bernanke, however, the FDIC has always been treated as a secondary regulator. Bair claimed she was often excluded from meetings or not informed of decisions at meetings that would affect her agency.

Bair made a surprising claim in her book, "Bull by the Horns" when she wrote that she had not been informed about SIVs until 2007. In 2007 Citi was the largest player in the $350 billion SIV market with seven funds totaling $80 billion. If you look at a list of the 50 largest banks at the time, a $350 billion bank would have been the fifth largest in the country after Wells Fargo Bank.

Bair wrote, "My first clue was the structured investment vehicle (SIV) fiasco, which occurred in August 2007. Citi and a few other large banks had set up SIV's as a way to invest in mortgages and mortgage-backed securities. For reasons that still today remain a mystery to me, they were allowed by the regulators – the Fed and the OCC – to keep the investments off-balance-sheet, meaning they were not included in the financial reports insured banks filed with us... indeed our examiners did not know anything about SIVs until the Federal Reserve Board alerted us to Citi"s difficulties."[3]

Certainly the Fed and the OCC had an obligation to communicate appropriately with the FDIC, but it seems to me she painted a picture of her agency that was out of it's league with the giant banks. The FASB ruling in 2003, regarding SIVs was hardly secret.

At one point during the discussion about what to do with Citigroup, she suggested that maybe Citi should be allowed to fail. She made the distinction between Citibank N.A. and the holding company Citigroup.

Paulson couldn't believe what she was saying. He said, "I'm having an out of body experience here, Sheila. I can't believe we're having this discussion. You're talking about Citigroup going through receivership."[4]

Paulson and Bernanke expressed frustration at times with what they described as Bair's myopic view.

Bair later said, "I was kind of tired of the attempts to provide special help to Citi. Both the Office of the Comptroller of the Currency (John Dugan) and the New York Fed's Tim Geithner refused to except the reality of just how sick the institution was she pointed out that even when city was on the verge of failure the OCC gave Citi a Camel Rating 3 (4 and 5 are troubled banks) and even after receiving TARP funds it remained a thinly capitalized bank."[5]

She believed Citi received special treatment because of Robert Rubin's role at Citi and Tim Geithner's role at the New York Fed. Citi's failure would reflect badly on both.

The Financial Crisis Inquiry Commission (FCIC) was very cautious in any criticism of Fannie and Freddie, but came down hard on the New York Fed and Tim Geitner. The Commission referred to an internal Federal Reserve Board document dated May 2005 which faulted the New York Fed for staffing it's Citigroup team" at a level that has not kept pace with a magnitude of supervisory issues the institution has realized."

The board in Washington has always been careful in criticizing one of its member banks especially the New York Fed. It was seemingly a mild rebuke but it is at the heart of federal bank examination and supervision.

Barry Ritholtz had a chart of Citigroup bailout which is worth repeating here:

"The deal is complex in its structure, but when all is said and done the government is on the hook for $249 billion in toxic mortgage-backed assets in exchange for $27 billion in Citi preferred stock paying 8 percent. Terms of the $306 billion in loans:

- The first $29 billion of losses from the portfolio will be absorbed by Citi entirely.
- The Treasury will take 90 percent of the next $5 billion of losses, with Citi taking the rest.
- The FDIC will step in and take 90 percent of the next $10 billion of losses while Citi absorbs the balances.

Losses beyond that will be taken by the Federal Reserve in 90 percent government role

The math: $306 billion in guarantees is:

$306 - 29 = 277 \times 0.90 = 249.3$ or $249.3 billion 3.

The above amount was in addition to the $45 billion TARP funds that Citi received.

Bailout Nation page 217.

Chapter 41

Dodd-Frank

The Dodd-Frank Wall Street Reform and Consumer Protection Act of 2010, also known as the Financial Stability Act or simply Dodd-Frank was passed in an all-night session. It's 2300 pages long and left open the need to write hundreds of new regulations.

Congress loves to give new legislation grand sounding names and in the process create new super councils or committees. The law was written in anger by politicians who were anxious to have their names on a bill that punished the greedy bankers.

Dodd-Frank is intended to prevent another financial crisis and address the problem of "too big to fail". It has some good provisions but it is doubtful it will prevent another financial crisis. At the heart of the legislation is something called the Financial Stability Oversight Council (FSOC).

The members of FSOC are:

- Secretary of the Treasury, Chair of FSOC
- Chair, Federal Reserve Board
- Comptroller of the Currency, OCC
- Chair, Federal Deposit Insurance Corporation, FDIC
- Chair Securities and Exchange Commission, SEC
- Director, Federal Housing Administration, FHA
- Chair, National Credit Union Administrator
- Director, Bureau of Consumer Finance Protection

- Chair, Commodities Futures Trading Commission, FTC
- An independent member with insurance expertise

In addition to the 10 member Council there is a five member advisory board. FSOC which could be described as a super advisory board has its own advisory board.

The Act also provides for a new Office of Financial Research in the Treasury Department. The Treasury and the Fed and the Fed member banks all have huge research departments.

Senator Durbin, who has been in Congress for over 30 years, the last 15 as a senator, has always been anti-bank. He offered a late amendment to Dodd-Frank that requires the Fed to set debit card transaction fees.

Whether you believe that this is price-fixing as many claim, or the right thing to do to protect protect bank customers, costs generally get passed on in some form, or if that is not possible, the service maybe denied to lower income customers.

Dodd—Frank has a section called "Living Wills, "which is very controversial. It requires large financial institutions to file a document with the Fed and the FDIC which demonstrates how the institutions non-bank affiliate could be wound down in a bankruptcy process without causing systemic disruption.

If the institution could not show that the nonbank operations could be solved in an orderly way the Fed and the FDIC working together (a new concept) would have the authority to step in and take what action is needed.

Is this a dramatic blueprint for action, or what? The FDIC record during the financial crisis was terrible. IndyMac and Washington Mutual were examples of incompetence. The agency didn't even know a $350 billion SIV market existed until they were "alerted by the Fed."

Section 113 states that a two thirds vote of the Council, to include the affirmative vote of the chair, may determine that if a non-bank financial company appears to be at risk it shall be referred to the Board of Governors of the Fed for supervision.

Although this section does not give FSOC any direct supervisory role, many believe it to be an important step in addressing the role of "shadow banking" in the financial crisis. I'm not sure the Fed Board of Governors are anxiously anticipating a heads up from FSOC about a nonbank financial company that they didn't know was in trouble.

Paul McCulley, CEO, of PIMCO, coined the term shadow banking system at an Economic Symposium held by the Fed at Jackson Hole, Wyoming, in 2007. He suggested that the birth of shadow banking originated with the money market funds in the early 1970s. Paul Krugman and others believe the shadow banking system was at the heart of what caused the financial crisis.

The non-bank financial companies that make up the system includes: money market funds, hedge funds, insurance companies and investment firms. All of these companies grew dramatically through derivatives like collateral debt obligations and credit default swaps. The funding for the system largely came from big banks like Citi, J.P. Morgan and Bank of America.

A major distinction between regional banks and money center banks is how they fund assets. Regional banks fund acquisitions mainly from insured deposit accounts. Generally the ratio is over 80 percent

Money center banks deposits supply a much smaller percentage, Citibank was an extreme example. Almost all of the funds these banks use to acquire assets comes from short-term funds like the Repo market.

Money market funds often pay higher rates on deposits then banks. Money market fund customers assumed the government would guarantee the funds and they were right.

Before TARP was available Paulson and Bernanke were looking for creative ways to lend money to the banks. However, the non-banks were a major problem. Paulson considered using the Exchange Stabilization Fund to bail out AIG. The fund was established in 1934 to be used to stabilize the dollar in international trade.

He eventually abandoned the idea as to much of a stretch. He later used the Fund to save the money market funds. After Bernanke bailed out AIG it was hoped the markets would stabilize. The DOW fell almost 500 points on September 17, 2008 to the lowest point in three years.

There was concern about the money funds but Paulson and Bernanke were stunned when they learned that the Reserve Primary Fund, one of the oldest and most highly regarded funds was in deep trouble. It was a $63 billion fund that had lost $785 million in Lehman Brothers short term paper.

Investors withdrew $20 billion in one day. The net asset value declined to under one dollar, known as breaking the buck.

Money market funds had grown from approximately $600 billion in 1992 to almost $4 trillion in 2009. The money market funds compete aggressively with banks for the most profitable customers, but do not pay FDIC fees or regulatory fees.

Paulson and Bernanke made an unprecedented change and decided to use government guarantees to bail out the money market funds. It was a complicated process but basically the Fed agreed to lend funds to the banks to buy short term paper from the Reserve Primary Fund and Paulson used the Exchange Stabilization Fund as a guarantee program.

The Fed came up with several other programs. The Term Auction Facility (TAF) was an alternative to the Discount Window. The Fed would lend up to 28 - 84 days on a wide range of collateral. In a few months time the total was $40 billion.

Another facility was is the Primary Dealer Credit Facility (PDCF). For the first time investment banks were allowed to borrow at the Discount Window. Non-investment grade bonds were accepted as collateral. Use of the facility allowed the Fed to conduct on-site examinations of companies regulated by the SEC.

Dodd-Frank and the Basel III committee had worked together to identify the Systemically Important Financial Institution (SIFIs) to set risk measurements and capital standards.

The Basel Committee began in 1974 as a group of central-bank governors from 20 countries to work on an international agreement for bank capital requirements. Basel I was not finalized until 1998. Basel III seems finalized but much of the decision-making in this country is passed onto FSOC.

The following is a list of the largest 10 financial companies in the group. The final list will have many more names and is subject to change:

		TRILLIONS OF DOLLARS
1.	BNP Paribus France	$3.20
2.	Royal Bank of Scotland	2.99
3.	Barclays U.K.	2.50
4.	Deutsche Bank Germany	2.43
5.	HSBK U.K.	2.42
6.	Credit Agricole	2.30
7.	Bank of America	2.09
8.	Mitsubishi Japan	2.07
9.	J P Morgan Chase	2.02
10.	UBS Switzerland	1.80
	Total	$23.82 TRILLION

When people say break up the big bank it's worth noting what the world competition looks like.

The following is a list of the largest US holding companies as of 9/10/2013.

			TRILLIONS
1.	J. B. Morgan Chase		$2.43
2.	Bank of America		2.129
3.	Citigroup		1.899
4.	Wells Fargo		1.488
		Sub Total	$7.979

			BILLIONS
5.	Goldman Sachs		$923
6.	Morgan Stanley		832
7.	AIG		541
8.	GE		528
		Sub Total	$2.824
Eight Company Total			$10.803 TRILLION

			BILLIONS
9.	BNY Mellon		$372
10.	U.S. Bancorp		360
11.	HSBC		309
12.	PNC		304
13.	Capital One Bank		290
14.	State Street		261
15.	TD Bank		231
16.	Principal Finance		201
		Sub Total	$2.283 Trillion
Total sixteen companies:			$23.82 Trillion

It's striking the four largest companies had approximately $8 trillion in assets, almost one third of the total of 16 holding companies. The size of the companies drop dramatically after the first eight companies.

Bashing bankers has always been good politics but anger, distrust and even hate was ratcheted up to a new level during the financial crisis. Both parties indulged in it. Senator John McCain has generally been scornful of bankers. Charlie Gasparino reported the following expletive exchange Senator McCain had when he was the Republican candidate for the presidency with Henry Paulson, "How the fuck can you trust them?"[1]

Joe Biden, shortly after being elected Vice President, said, referring to bankers, "I'd like to throw some of these guys in the Brig. They're thinking the same old thing that got us here, greed."[2]

I guess the Vice President used the term brig rather than prison because he had recently moved into the Naval Observatory residence.

In March 2009, President Obama gave a speech at a Town Hall meeting in Cosa Mesa, California, where he compared bankers to suicide bombers. He said, "It's almost like they've got a bomb strapped to them and they've got their hands on the trigger. You don't want them to blow up, but you got to kind of talk to them, to ease that finger off the trigger."

It was a jarring analogy, suicide bombers were blowing up innocent women and children in restaurants and school buses in the Mideast.

The President went on to excoriate officials at AIG for their greed and recklessness and he paused and said, "Excuse me… I'm choked up with anger."[3]

After telling his audience they had a right to be angry with him, he said he wanted to channel their anger in a constructive way. Channeling anger and distrust in a constructive way is very difficult.

When I was confronted with demonstrators, I realized it was impossible to talk to a group of picketers and probably foolish to try. However, I did talk to quite a few who left their signs outside and came into the bank.

The anger directed at me was disturbing but what really was upsetting was that most of them had little knowledge of the facts that caused the demonstration and they had no desire to listen. Their anger overwhelmed any dialogue.

The distrust of bankers is now so embedded in our society I wonder what might happen if we have another financial crisis? Will the Congress and the public say we're tired of bailing these guys out, it's time for the government to take over the banking system?

Think about how our entire banking system was nationalized by Henry Paulson with a three page bill. Not just the bad banks but all the good banks, too. It's fortunate that the bill was structured so the recipients of TARP could pay the funds back and escape government control of the business.

We should think carefully before accepting the idea that "big banks" are a menace to our financial system. Sheila Bair, who lived through the crisis said Dodd-Frank oversight should be a powerful weapon to prevent banks from becoming too big.

If you look at the list of the "big nine" institutions that were described as systemically important, two of the four biggest, JP Morgan Chase and Wells Fargo were never in trouble and didn't need government funds. Bank of America was shaky but clearly not insolvent like Citibank.

Goldman Sachs and Morgan Stanley were at risk because of AIG, a non-bank. Once AIG was off the table both companies were healthy!

State Street and BNY Mellon are not traditional banks. They exited the business earlier when they sold their Retail and Commercial Loan Divisions. They received modest funding (if you call billions modest)and quickly resumed the status of well capitalized institutions.

The ability of a bank to withstand a run depends on sufficient capital and good risk management practices. However, no bank can withstand wholesale runs triggered by external events that causes panicked withdrawals by depositors or in the recent crisis by panicked withdrawals of short term institutional lenders.

The randomness of outside events may have nothing to do with institutions being too big. As we have seen the randomness and unpredictability of human behavior is difficult to predict with mathematical models.

Irving Fisher was a Yale professor who was intrigued with mathematics. His PhD dissertation was titled, "Mathematical Investigations in the Theory of Value and Price." Paul Samuelson said it was "the greatest doctoral dissertation in economics ever written."

Fisher accumulated considerable wealth through his investments but strangely enough his most profitable ideas came from his invention of the Rolodex in 1910.

Before the crash of 1929.he saw the roaring stock market is an indication of the "new era of permanent prosperity." He said the new Federal Reserve would avert any future depression or monetary crisis.

On Monday, October 16, 1929, less than two weeks before the crash, in may be an immortal prediction, Fisher said, "that stock market prices have reached what looks like a permanently high plateau.[4]

The legendary John Maynard Keynes told his friend the Swiss banker Felix Somary in 1926, that it was a good time to buy stocks. He firmly declared, "we will not have any more crashes in our time."[5]

We had the Stock Market Crash and the Great Depression. We also had the worst bank run in our history that had little to do with two big to fail.

I wrote about Penn Square bank earlier. One of the interesting things about Penn Square was that small obscure bank failure led to a panic and an eventual significant change in monetary policy.

President Jimmy Carter appointed Nancy Teeters as the first woman governor of the Federal Reserve Board in 1978. She quickly proved to be an outstanding member of the board.

After the failure of Penn Square she said, "here is a bank located in a shopping center in Oklahoma City that nobody's heard of before and all of a sudden no one is sure what will happen next. She went on to say, "after the Penn Square failure, I began to get the feeling we might be heading towards something we hadn't seen since the 1930s.[6]

I realize Penn Square didn't happen in isolation, the Continental Illinois failure followed and savings and loan problems were escalating but Penn Square was so significant it caused Nancy Teeters and several FOMC colleagues to ask Paul Volcker to ease monetary policy.

After the government took over Fannie and Freddie the implied guarantee quickly became a full guarantee of both Fannie and Freddie's obligations. As the crisis deepened and spread across the entire financial system, the government agreed to guarantee just about every company deemed vital to the economy except Lehman Brothers.

During the intense discussions about distributing TARP funds, one of the most contentious items was that Paulson, Bernankee and Geihtner wanted the FDIC to guarantee all deposits. Bair firmly resisted but finally agreed to insure all bank deposits.

When the agreement was reached David Nason, one of Paulson's inner circle, said, "the full guarantee represents the biggest policy shift in history."[7]

Henry Paulson wrote about the regulatory system from very personal experience. "Our regulatory system remains a hopelessly outmoded patch work quilt built for another day and age. It is rife with duplication, gaping holes, and competition among regulators. The system hasn't kept pace with financial innovation and needs to be fixed so that we have the capacity and the authority to respond to a constantly evolving global capital market."[8]

Chapter 42

Abolish The OCC And The FDIC

State Street Corporation and State Street Bank are good examples of the over lap and duplication of bank supervision and why the system should be scrapped and restructured. The 2012 annual report states:

"We conduct our business primarily through State Street Bank, which traces its beginnings to 1792," (more than 100 years before the Federal Reserve was established.) "State Street Bank's current charter was authorized by a Special Act of the Massachusetts legislature in 1891 and the present name was adopted in 1960. State Street Bank operates as a trust custody bank."

In 1969 State Street Corporation was formed; the bank holding company is subject to the laws of Massachusetts and the Bank Holding Company Act of 1956. Regulation and supervision of the holding company is subject to the Federal Reserve, specifically the Federal Reserve Bank of Boston.

In the late 1990s State Street exited traditional banking and sold its retail and commercial divisions to Citizens Bank in Rhode Island. State Street currently has two lines of business: Investment Servicing and Investment Management. It is the largest provider of mutual fund custody and accounting services in the United States.

State Street Bank is chartered by the Commonwealth of Massachusetts and is subject to supervision by the Commissioner of Banks. South Shore Bank, when I was CEO, was a state chartered Bank and we were examined by the Massachusetts Banking Department. Examiners were professional, experienced and very fair. However, South Shore Bank was a traditional Community Bank. State Street is a complex financial company that has nothing to do with the Massachusetts Banking Department.

State Street has been designated "a global systemically important financial institution (SIFI)" or G-SIB by Dodd-Frank. It's in a unique class of global financial institutions. In addition to Dodd-Frank there are many federal laws that apply.

State Street's broker/dealer subsidiary comes under SEC rules, the London Stock Exchange, Deutsche Boerse Ag, and Bank of Japan. The other non U.S. servicing operations come under the Fed's Regulation K through State Street Bank's Edge Act subsidiary.

Various subsidiary trust companies are subject to supervision by the Office of the Comptroller of the Currency. State Street's 2012 report listed regulation fees and assessments at $53 million.

The Full Employment and Balanced Growth Act of 1978 is better known as the Humphrey–Hawkins Act. It is named for the late Senator Hubert Humphrey. The act requires the Chair of the Federal Reserve to report to Congress twice a year and explain what the Fed is doing through monetary policy to reduce unemployment and control inflation. You can imagine how exciting those sessions are.

Unfortunately there is no requirement to report on the health of the financial companies the Fed supervises so there is little personal accountability.

The Federal Reserve does not publish an annual report which also is unfortunate. However, I found it interesting to read the Federal Reserve Bank of Boston's annual reports for 2008 and 2009.

In reading the 2008 report you would never know we had just experienced the worst recession since the Great Depression and TARP was not even mentioned. The 2009 report did not mention TARP or the Stimulus. Eric Rosengren, president and chief executive officer, did write the following about how they are "reconsidering the nation's financial regulatory framework."

"With the financial crisis ebbing in 2009 we worked hard to parse out and apply, it's lessons. We are, for example, reorienting our bank supervisory activities in areas like capital adequacy, risk management practices, liquidity management, and the effects on risk-taking of compensation structures. And we are augmenting traditional firm-specific oversight with a more comprehensive approach to anticipating and addressing threats of financial stability –a so-called "macroprudential" approach that goes beyond a focus on the safety and soundness of individual institutions to also focus on risks to the financial system as a whole."

I have not met Eric Rosengren, but I understand he is highly regarded by the Federal Reserve community. I wish however, he and other Fed officials would stop writing things like they are in some academic Wonderland.

The Office of the Comptroller of the Currency, (OCC) is a huge federal agency that was created during the Civil War as part of the Treasury. Most of the largest banks in the country have national charters and are regulated by the OCC. All national banks are required to be members of the Federal Reserve.

I wrote earlier that state-chartered banks almost disappeared during the Civil War, but after the introduction of deposit banking there was a great resurgence of state banks. Membership in the Fed was optional and many community banks opted not to belong. A number of the largest banks in the country like Chase chose not to belong.

The Comptroller of the Currency is appointed by the President to a five-year term and the Comptroller reports to the Secretary of the Treasury. As such, the Comptroller is viewed by many as part of the Executive Branch. The position does not have the prestige and recognition that the Chairman of the Federal Reserve enjoys. The Fed regularly tries to exert it's authority.

There have been several colorful Comptrollers in the past who have been willing to challenge the Fed. One was James Saxon, who was appointed by President Kennedy. Saxon served in the 1960s and his rulings were often challenged by the Fed. Saxon completely ignored the Fed restrictions.

Martin Mayer had an interesting anecdote about how Saxon was liberating national banks from regulatory constraints and driving the Fed crazy. "Citibank, a nationally chartered Fed member was out there pushing the envelope and Chase, a state-chartered Fed member was being held down." "Walter Wriston of Citibank, remembered a meeting of the International Monetary Conference... The vice-chairman of the Fed announced that his board would never allow this sort of thing Saxon was permitting. David Rockefeller, (the Chase CEO), went down to Washington right after the meeting and applied for a national charter after saying he thought Saxon was crazy."[1]

I met James Saxon years ago at a banking convention at the Mount Washington Hotel in New Hampshire. By chance I had an interesting lunch with him. After lunch he said, "I would like to show you my new car." It certainly didn't stand out in the parking lot. It was a nondescript, rather old looking vehicle. He said it was great fun out-running a police car that tried to stop him. He raised the hood and showed me a beautiful new engine that must have come out of a high-end car. I don't remember whether it was a Porsche or something else, but it was magnificent!

In more recent times the Comptrollers have been a lot less flamboyant than Saxon and hardly even noticed in the financial press. I looked back at more than a dozen books written about the financial crisis and John Dugan, who as Comptroller at the time was not even mentioned.

The OCC is located in Washington, D.C. and has four district offices in New York, Chicago, Dallas and Denver and an office in London. There are 48 field offices.

It's not well known but the OCC began using "resident examiners" in the biggest banks in the mid 1980's. The number of resident examiners was substantially increased after 2007. Several of the biggest banks had as many as 60 full-time examiners in residence. The OCC had 626 resident examiners in it's Large Banks Supervision Group.

The Federal Reserve Bank of New York also uses teams of resident examiners. The OCC and Fed examiners have access to computer programs and they attend various management meetings and some board meetings.

In spite of on-site scrutiny by the OCC and the Fed, Citibank and Bank of America, two of the largest banks in the country, were allowed to run with little oversight.

John Dugan is a Republican lawyer who was appointed by President George H.W. Bush to Assistant Secretary of Domestic Affairs at the Treasury in 1985 where he served until 1989.

Later President George W. Bush appointed him to Comptroller of the Currency in 2005. Dugan was reappointed to serve until September 2010. He served in that critical position during the financial crisis. Dugan is not well-known like Paulson or Bernanke, but he had a major role in drafting the TARP legislation.

The Comptroller of the Currency also is a Director of the FDIC. Dugan and Bair had a testy relationship which Sheila Bair covers in some detail in her book "Bull by the Horns." Dugan chaired the Basel Committee from 2007–2009 which worked on international bank regulation which also caused conflict with Bair.

Chairman Bair wrote, "Let's face it, the OCC failed miserably in its mandate of ensuring the safety and soundness of the national banks it regulates." Her anger was so great she recommended abolishing the OCC and letting the FDIC supervise all banks and the Fed supervise bank holding companies and nonbank systemic financial institutions.

It's a good recommendation in part but actually the FDIC's record wasn't any better during the crisis.

In August 2009, after Armageddon had been adverted, Mr. Dugan made the following classic statement about the role of the OCC in bank regulation to a Senate Banking Committee hearing. "Our experience at OCC has been that effective, integrated safety and soundness and compliance supervision grows from detailed core knowledge that our examiners develop and maintain about each bank's business lines, products, services customer base and level of risk, knowledge and expertise through on site examinations and contact with our community banks and close day to day focus on the activities of larger banks."

It was an elegant statement, but the senators knew it was completely detached from reality. Citigroup had been bailed out three times while most of them had been in office.

I mentioned the professional bank examinations we had at South Shore Bank by the Massachusetts Banking Department. There is a world of difference between an examination at South Shore Bank or Bank of New Hampshire and Citibank, or any of the giant banks.

I hadn't been at Bank of New Hampshire, a national bank, very long when the head OCC examiner said to me, "you did okay at State Street but you haven't proven anything here yet." I thought it was a little amusing that we actually were paying his salary. We got along just fine and it was an uneventful examination. I doubt the OCC examiner would say something like that to Robert Rubin at Citigroup, nor would he have the same day to day contact with Sandy Weill or Rubin that I had and enjoyed with the bank examiners.

I suspect that a lot of the problems leading up to the crisis were not so much the fault of the examiners as it was from the reluctance at the top to take required action.

Certainly the examination of a giant bank requires different skills and experience from the examination of a community bank or regional bank. However, the lessons learned from recent experience should be a blueprint for the future.

It's important that non-bank financial companies have some form of federal regulation but the banks shouldn't pay for it. The Fed, OCC and FDIC are paid out of bank fees by the members.

I don't think we should continue to separate supervision between bank holding companies and the subsidiary banks. Citigroup, the holding company, was supervised by the New York Fed and Citibank, the subsidiary, was supervised by the OCC.

Epilogue

"The farther backward you look, the farther forward you are likely to see." Winston Churchill

To my family and friends who were kind enough to ask me how my book was coming along, knowing I would tell them in more detail then they wanted, I thank you for your patience and encouragement. To those who may have stumbled across my writing and are thinking this is really old news and I should move on, I can only say Fannie and Freddie are not old news.

Fannie and Freddie are still owned by the tax-payers and remain the dominant players in the home mortgage market. The mortgages they own and guarantee depend on economic conditions, including house prices. The positive reports of their return to profitability should be viewed in the context that they are subsidized government enterprises.

Federal Housing Finance Agency Director Lockhart said Fannie and Freddie will continue to be able to purchase conforming mortgages without restraint and the government is continuing to buy 60 percent of all home mortgage loans today.

When I began writing more than two years ago I had definite ideas about the mortgage market and the federal government's role in the housing market, however as I was writing and doing extensive research I found some of my ideas were incomplete and needed to be updated.

I supported George W. Bush as President but I am dismayed to have to admit he encouraged and supported many of the same housing policies that President Clinton initiated, all of which eventually brought Fannie and Freddie to ruin. Although Bush lacked several of the colorful and aggressive activists in the Clinton Administration, his HUD secretaries Mel Martinez and Alphonso Jackson acted like Clinton appointees.

Every president in modern times has embraced higher rates of home ownership for Americans. George W. Bush probably was reacting to the charge that he was a rich uncaring Republican, but his attempt to have both higher rates of ownership and restraint of Fannie and Freddie was not possible.

Bush supported several attempts to pass legislation to curtail the high-risk lending of both GSE's and also legislation that would have strengthened regulation and oversight by a new federal agency as part of the Treasury Department. Unfortunately he was unable to gain sufficient congressional support.

Within the first several years of his presidency he received a letter from 76 members of Congress, including Nancy Pelosi, Barney Frank, Maxine Waters and Charlie Rangel warning him that his focus on safety and soundness would do damage to affordable housing programs.

During my research I examined again Federal housing legislation. The Civil Rights Act of 1968, also known as the Fair Housing Act; the Community Reinvestment Act 1977 (CRA) with the major changes through 2005; The Equal Credit Opportunity Act 1974; The Home Mortgage Disclosure Act 1975, (HMDA); and the Federal Safety and Soundness Act 1992, known as the GSE Act.

In spite of living with these laws during my working years and being in some peril if I did not I was surprised I had overlooked the major role the Department of Housing and Urban Development (HUD) played in pushing Fannie and Freddie into ever increasing risky mortgage loans to satisfy HUD mandated goals for affordable housing. The goals could only be met if both GSE's drastically reduced their traditional underwriting standards.

It is a critical part of the story of why Freddie and Fannie failed and it has been deliberately buried or excused by the people in government who were most responsible for causing the failure of the two GSE's.

I have written at length about Fannie and Freddie and the special benefits they both received as government-sponsored enterprises and continue to receive as wholly-owned Government companies.

In spite of the voluminous information available about Fannie and Freddie many financial writers continue to downplay the significant role they both played in the financial crisis.

The truth is five years after government takeover both GSE's are still wards of the government and they continue to borrow funds from the treasury at special rates and have a government guarantee of their obligations.

At the peak of the bubble there were over 53 million mortgage loans with outstanding balances of over $9 trillion. Fannie and Freddie accounted for approximately $5 trillion of the amount. The American Enterprise Institute estimated that Fannie and Freddie's mortgage portfolio contained in excess of $2 trillion of subprime loans.

On Sunday, September 7, 2008, Secretary of the Treasury Henry Paulson, announced that the government had placed Fannie and Freddie into conservatorship. If the company had gone through a bankruptcy preceding the losses on mortgage loans and mortgage-backed securities would have been horrendous.

The Federal Housing Finance Regulatory Reform Act of 2008 provided the legislation to restructure Fannie and Freddie under a new federal agency, the Federal Housing Finance Agency, (FHFA).

Among the positive things that came out of the legislation was neither company could use taxpayer funds for lobbying. Between 1998 and 2008 the two companies had spent $174 million on lobbying.

Once the restructuring of Fannie and Freddie was in place Paulson was still faced with two government owned companies that were insolvent and continuing to lose billions of dollars.

Paulson's first $700 billion bailout plan, on three pages, included wording that turned Paulson into an Economic Czar. The following are the powers he was asking Congress for, "Decisions by the Secretary pursuant to the authority of this Act are non- reviewable and committed to agency discretion, and may not be reviewed by any court of law or any administrative agency."

Paulson was not only asking for the biggest bailout in history he was putting himself beyond the reach of Congress. Obviously it did not go over well. Senator Chris Dodd said, "after reading this proposal, I can only conclude that it is not only our economy that is at risk, Mr. Secretary, but our constitution as well."

Paulson's draft of the legislation was deemed unacceptable and he went back to the drawing board, but it was an indication of his boldness and confidence.

Although Paulson removed the section that appointed him the Economic Czar from his bill, on September 29th, the House of Representatives voted down his bailout bill by a narrow margin.

A number of economists and members of Congress accepted the idea of dire consequences if something substantial was not done, however, many were not convinced another Great Depression was at hand.

The politicians increasingly were responding to a sense of panic from their constituents which were fueled by horror stories in the press of Armageddon if they didn't do something.

Paulson wrote in his book, "On the Brink," how one of his closest advisors, Dan Jester, and Bob Scully of Morgan Stanley came up with the idea of using a Keepwell agreement, which is a contract between a parent company and a subsidiary in which the parent guarantees that it will provide necessary financing for the subsidiary.

The Treasury's Keepwell Agreement was known as the Preferred Stock Purchase Agreement. The Treasury was allowed to advance funds to the GSE's to maintain a positive net worth no matter how much they lost in the future.

Paulson said, "By entering into that agreement before December 31, 2009 (when our temporary authority expired) we would be acting within our authority, while providing investors the necessary long term assurances. As losses were realized in the future, we could dip into the Keepwell and increase the amount of financial support by purchasing preferred shares."

The next question was how big should the Keepwell be considering they were nearing the debt ceiling. Paulson asked for $100 billion to maintain positive capital positions.

After Bush and Paulson left office President Obama raised the caps to $200 billion and on Christmas Eve, Timothy Geithner, Obama's Secretary of the Treasury, quietly removed the caps.

It's interesting that several years after the crisis all of the large banks and most of the smaller banks have paid back the government funds with interest and all of the large banks, except Citigroup, have passed the new "Stress Tests."

What is often overlooked and generally not known by the public is the real bailout at Fannie and Freddie involved a massive buying program of Fannie's and Freddie's mortgage-backed securities.

Quantitative Easing 1 began on November 25, 2008 and ended on March 3, 2010. During that relatively short period of time the Fed bought $1.25 trillion of mortgage-backed securities. Ginnie Mae and the Federal Home Loan Banks were included in the program but the bulk of the purchases were from Fannie and Freddie.

The need for Fannie and Freddie to ask the government for additional capital injections was greatly reduced by ridding their balance sheets of billions of dollars of toxic securities.

The bailout of Fannie and Freddie was not "just" $150 billion, it was in the range of $1 trillion.

There were two other companies that were insolvent in September 2008 and were bailed out by the government. American International Group (AIG) and Citigroup.

AIG was different from Fannie and Freddie, but the government was responsible for allowing the Financial Products Group of AIG to run like a giant hedge fund with virtually no government regulation.

Brooksley Born, Head of the Commodities Futures Trading Commission, (CFTC) proposed legislation to regulate derivatives, especially credit default swaps CDS, which were at the heart of AIG's downfall.

Robert Rubin, and Larry Summers at the Treasury Department, with the help of Senator Phil Gramm, a powerful Republican Head of the Senate Banking Committee, blocked any legislation regarding CDSs.

Treasury Secretary Rubin had a legitimate reason for caution at a critical time in the economy but that does not excuse the government for not recognizing and fixing the problem before it became a crisis.

After Lehman went bankrupt on September 14, three days later AIG had to be bailed out with a $85 billion investment by the Fed. Shortly after, AIG received $100 billion from TARP.

As I wrote earlier, once AIG was rescued, Goldman Sachs and Morgan Stanley were able to raise substantial new capital and in late September both became bank holding companies.

During the same period of financial upheaval and uncertainty, Bank of America closed the deal to acquire Merrill Lynch. Bank of America shares were selling at $34 a share and it was an all stock transaction. The approximate price for Merrill was $50 billion, and a few months later Bank of America stock was selling for $13 per share, reducing the value of the acquisition to about $19 billion.

Ken Lewis, CEO of Bank of America, had acquired Countrywide earlier in the year for $4 billion. Both acquisitions, but especially Merrill, would cause serious losses depleting Bank of America's capital and further eroding the stock price. Ken Lewis would soon be out of Bank of America.

I have written at length about Citigroup and the massive government bailout. Here is a brief recap: Citi received $45 billion from TARP and a government guarantee of $300 billion in toxic loans and securities. The guarantee amount projected a net risk to the government of $250 billion.

Although Bank of America was one of the largest banks in the country and had to be bailed out, like Citi, it received $45 billion, however it was Fannie and Freddie, Citi, and AIG that were insolvent in 2008 and on the brink of catastrophic failure.

The government bears significant responsibility for the more than $1 trillion bailout of these four companies.

I realize that Americans live very busy lives and wading through the information on the Financial Crisis is a formidable task, however if we don't pay attention to what happened we will have only ourselves to blame when they do the same things again.

After I wrote this last paragraph and decided to end my book, I was stunned to read two speeches by Shaun Donovan, President Obama's Secretary of HUD and learn how he plans to use discrimination and racism to mount another housing crusade.

Donovan spoke in a Treasury Conference on housing in 2010 and he said, "Fannie and Freddie facilitated the democratization of credit and we witnessed dramatic growth in ownership among underserved groups." He added, "the desire to increase profits drove Fannies and Freddie's increased appetite for risk, not government mandates to support affordable housing. We should not learn the wrong lesson from that experience."

Donovan's remarks contained partial truths but left out essential facts. When he said Fannie's and Freddie's appetite for increased risk was for profits and not because of government mandates, he left out that a major reason for increased profits was for executive bonuses which were reached through fraudulent bookkeeping.

He also did not mention that his predecessors at HUD, Henry Cisneros and Andrew Cuomo, in the Clinton administration, set increased goals for affordable housing from 42 percent to 50 percent.

President Bush, soon after he was elected in 2001, was urged by holdovers from his predecessor to increase affordable housing goals from 50 percent to 57 percent; Bush agreed to 56 percent. One of the many problems has always been to agree on a definition of "Affordable Housing."

Donovan's praise for the dramatic growth in ownership among the underserved groups did not acknowledge that the peak in homeownership at just under 70 percent has since declined to pre-Clinton era levels.

Donovan used the phrase "democratization of credit." It is a phase that was frequently used by Eugene Ludwig, who served as Controller of the Currency in the Clinton Administration.

Democratization of credit sounds nice but it really means re-allocation of credit to borrowers who may not meet traditional requirements.

Ludwig aggressively supported CRA and used 2,400 national bank examiners, including undercover shoppers, to find biased lenders.

Paul Sperry wrote, "These days, Ludwig is advising the Obama Administration on ways to turn the CRA into a more potent weapon against the financial industry. At a minimum, the CRA should be brought in to cover credit unions and insurance companies. Ideally, it should include all other major financial institutions, such as hedge funds and private equity funds."[1]

On July 16, 2013, Secretary Donovan gave a speech to the104[th] Annual Convention of the NAACP in Orlando, Florida. Unfortunately his remarks have received little media coverage or response from members of Congress.

Although his speech was lacking in detail it clearly suggests the implementation of an unprecedented level of social engineering, much of which appears to be a repeat of the affordable housing mistakes of a few years ago, plus a new level of enforcement by HUD.

He began by saying the administration will inform every neighborhood in the country if they don't have enough minorities living in their communities. He said "HUD is enhancing its enforcement techniques by initiating investigations on our own without waiting for individuals to file complaints.... For the first time ever HUD is providing information, data, to every single neighborhood in the nation detailing what access African American families and other members of protected classes have to community assets that I am talking about—jobs, schools, transit."

Donovan made the following pathetic remark about the lack of opportunity in America, "Unfortunately in too many of our hardest hit communities—no matter how hard a child works or her parents work, the life chances of that child, even her lifespan, is determined by the ZIP Code she grows up in."

Does he mean that HUD will create maps of housing and social composition by neighborhood and withhold federal funds if he is not satisfied with the mix? Perhaps he has in mind forced integration through government housing. He did say, "HUD is working to strengthen our stewardship of federal dollars to maximize the impact they have on communities in advancing fair housing goals."

Donovan referred to a future where ladders of opportunity are available to all Americans. The administration is adding three new ladders:

One: Stepping Up Fair Housing Enforcement. He of course referred to the fair housing Act 1968. His words echo everything we heard leading up to the housing collapse.

Question, "Will credit be limited to the few or the available to the many?"

Question," Will housing be limited to the few or available to the many?

Donovan challenged Congress, "we need to ensure all Americans have access to home ownership and can keep it.

Two: Access and Protection of Home Ownership

He said, "while blatant in-your-face discrimination is very real today, a quieter form of discrimination has emerged that is just as harmful to this country. That's why I want to send a message to all outside these doors. There are no stones we won't turn. There are no places we won't go."

Three: Building The Hardest Hit Neighborhoods

President Obama laid out a plan called Promise Zones in which his administration will partner with communities most impacted by the economic crisis.

Donovan said HUD will play a significant role in the "housing piece" through "Choice Neighborhoods." A redevelopment program through subsidized housing"

The president said it will be a key part of his 2014 budget.

Americans are very generous and most of us support the idea there are people who need a hand up to realize their full potential, however we have not fully recovered from the worst recession since the Great Depression. The cost has been enormous and we should not repeat the same mistakes again.

The irony is the ones who benefited the most from the largess of Fannie were executives like James Johnson, Franklin Raines and Jamie Gorlick, each of whom received compensation in the range of $100 million. Members of Congress also received huge campaign contributions and special favors; the millions of Americans who were supposed to be helped by government affordable housing programs in the end were the ones most hurt.

I WROTE THE FOLLOWING FOR OUR COMPANY NEWSPAPER "SHORELINES" A FEW MONTHS AFTER DEE BROWN WAS MISTAKENLY ARRESTED AS A BANK ROBBER.

Several years ago June and I had one of those wonderfully memorable vacations skiing with a group of friends in Austria. The days were bright and beautiful, there was enough natural snow, and being more the Bretton Woods kind of skiers than downhill racers, we were happy to find that not only was it the great thrill we expected, we actually survived! Drinking German beer and singing songs with old friends and new friends wasn't bad, either.

Late in the week, having grown a little leg weary, it seemed prudent to take a day to do some sightseeing. Most of the group spent the day in Innsbruck, but we decided to drive to Munich and also visit Dachau, just outside of Munich.

A number of the most notorious concentration camps were in Poland, but there in the heart of beautiful Bavaria, only miles from one of the most charming cities in Europe, was the first and one of the worst Nazi death camps. The camp is preserved at Dachau as a stark reminder of the atrocities committed during the Nazi regime.

I didn't go out of morbid curiosity, you can see as much as you want of the horrors of the Second World War on video in your living room; I went because in the midst of good fun and good fortune, it's important to remember the Holocaust did happen.

Someday I suspect the Germans and the Poles will tire of gruesome reminders like Dachau and Auschwitz and they will be bulldozed and grassed over. We should not forget, however, that the dark side of man exists in every culture in every community and it appears and grows if enough good people aren't willing to speak out and demand that it stop.

There has been an alarming increase in the number of hate crimes that have occurred in the communities we live in. Television news reports and the newspapers are filled with terrible stories of attacks on our neighbors simply because they are perceived to be different.

We should all feel threatened and repulsed by acts of violence against a member of the Asian community in Quincy or the desecration of the synagogue in Sharon or any one of the acts that reflect hate and bigotry in our communities. We should not remain silent.

Acknowledgements

To June, it has been a great journey together and I know a book would never have emerged from my written scribbles without your love and dedication.

To Laurel and Rusty, having read my book and lived through my banking life again, thank you and your beautiful families for making your mother and me very proud.

I realized when I began writing acknowledgments that I owe almost everyone I know my thanks for their patience and encouragement for listening to endless discussions about "the book."

I owe a special thanks to the following for their valuable input and help in completing the manuscript: Tom Hyman, for editing the book and making corrections and constructive suggestions. Also, for the many phone calls that were not part of the editing agreement.

To P.J. O'Rourke, thank you for reading the manuscript and taking a personal interest in discussions with my wife and me about publishing the book. Your support and encouragement is greatly appreciated.

To my former colleagues thank you for the great times we had together and providing the information and documents I neglected to keep and found I badly needed: Frank Belcastro, Pat Collura, Ed Furber, Jay Olin, Judy Peffer and Graham Waiting.

My sincere thanks to Joseph L. Hooley, Chief Executive Officer, and Patrick Centanni, Executive Vice President, State Street Corporation, for personally responding to my request for historical information and photographs of State Street Bank.

Jack McCarthy, my friend of more than 40 years and former colleague at State Street Bank and Bank of New Hampshire, thank you for reading

300 pages and offering needed corrections about people and places and your unfailing encouragement.

To Tom Streba, for living with my work for many months and listening to my stories and conclusions about the Financial Crisis. Thank you also for your support and encouragement.

To Sandy Cram, retired from the Federal Reserve Bank of Boston, thank you for sending copies of the current Federal Reserve Act, and copies of the "Mortgage Lending in Boston." "Interpreting HMDA Data" and "Closing the Gap."

To Roland Goodbody, Manuscripts Curator, University of New Hampshire, for giving me access to the late Sen. Thomas McIntyre's archives - especially his service on the Banking Committee during the 1970s Now Account hearings and legislation.

To Willard Williams, owner of the Toadstool Bookstore in Peterborough, New Hampshire, my thanks for your generous consultations about book publishing and book selling and to Diane Hiatt, Sarah Smith, and Robert DeGroff at Author House, many thanks for getting us to the final steps of publishing!

Notes

CHAPTER 13: THE BOSTON FED GOES ROGUE

1. Alicia Munnell, This study eliminates all other possible factors that could be influencing mortgage discussion"quotation by Paulette Thomas, "Boston Fed Finds Racial Discrimination in Mortgage Lending Still Widespread" Wall Street Journal, October 9, 1992
2. Federal Reserve Board of Governors published "Working Paper" The Role of Race in Mortgage Lending, Revisiting the Boston Fed Study" December 1996
3. David Horne, an economist with the FDIC, Financial Services Research" November
4. Gary Becker, Nobel Laureate, "RE flaws in all studies of discrimination" quoted by Peter Schweizer, "Architects of Ruin"

Chapter 14: COMMUNITY REINVESTMENT ACT

1. Paul Sperry "The Unauthorized Report About What Really Caused the Recession"
2. Heidi Schwartz, Assistant Professor, Rutgers University, University of Minnesota Press, p 86 "Organizing Urban America "Secular and Faith-based Progressive Movements" 2008
3. Quote by Andrew Cuomo, "House of Cards, A Tale of Hubris and Wretched Excess on Wall Street" William D. Cohan
4. Quote by Roberta Achtenberg "Don't Blame the Community Re-investment Act" American Prospect, June 26, 2009
5. Ellen Seidman, "CRA in the 21st Century" Mortgage Banker, October 1999
6. Seidman, "Lowering the Wealth Hurdle" Mortgage Banker
7. Peter Schweitzer, "Architects of Ruin" Paul Hancock, Deputy Attorney General DOJ

8. Peter Schweitzer quote Wells Fargo
9. Paul Sperry "The Great American Bank Robbery" The Federal Financial Institutions Examination Council
10. Sheila Bair, Chairman FDIC, "Bull By the Horns"
11. Bair
12. Roger Lowenstein "The The End of Wall Street" p33, Melissa Martinez, Chief Compliance Officer, Washington Mutual quote

CHAPTER 16: JOHN KERRY

1. J.P. Morgan quote during Pujo Committee Hearings, Ron Chernow "The House of Morgan"

CHAPTER 21: THE FEDERAL RESERVE

1. Paul Warburg, Kuhn Loeb, creator of the Federal Reserve from "The Federal Reserve" "The Creature From Jekyll Island" G. Edward Griffin"
2. Representative Barney Frank quote, David Wessel "In the Fed We Trust"

CHAPTER 22: THE SAVINGS INDUSTRY DISAPPEARS

1. Toby Roth testimony Congressional Hearing regarding Charles Keating, Lincoln Savings and Loan, Martin Mayer "The Greatest Bank Robbery Ever" "The Collapse of the Savings and Loan Industry
2. Martin Mayer, Trish Cosgrove, whistle blower

CHAPTER 23: THE TWINS: FANNIE AND FREDDIE

1. Barry Ritholtz "Bailout Nation"

CHAPTER 24: JAMES JOHNSON

1. Richard Stevenson, "The Velvet Fist of Fannie Mae," Johnson quote. New York Times, April 20, 1997
2. "Fannie Mae Moves to Aid Affordable Housing Loans" Washington Times, October 25, 2005
3. "Architects of Ruin," Peter Schweitzer, illegal immigrants
4. Quote by Heidi Swartz, Assistant Professor, Rutgers University, "Reaching the Immigrant Market" p50, Georgetown University Press

CHAPTER 25: FRANKLIN RAINES

1. Raines quote, "Financial Fiasco" Johan Norberg
2. Steven Holmes quote, New York Times, September 30, 1999, "Fannie Eases Credit to Aid of Mortgage Lending"

CHAPTER 26: PRESIDENT GEORGE W. BUSH

1. President Bush speech 2002 quoted in Thomas Sowell "The Housing Boom and Bust" p95, "Light where there is darkness"
2. Bush speech "I have issued a challenge" in Mortgage News Service, November 15, 2002, quoted by Thomas Sowell at White House Conference on Housing
3. Paul Sperry "The Great American Bank Robbery" chart
4. Paul Sperry
5. Treasury Secretary John Snow quote in "Reckless Endangerment" Gretchen Morgenson
6. Congressman Maxine Waters quote "Reckless Endangerment"

CHAPTER 27: SECURITIZATION

1. Lowell Bryan quote regarding securitization. "Bankers" Martin Mayer
2. Roger Lowenstein, "The End of Wall Street" quoting Alan Greenspan about derivatives
3. Charles Gasparino, "The Sellout"
4. Citigroup structured-investment vehicles Paul Muolo, Mathew Padilla, "Chain of Blame"
5. Naked credit default swaps described by Edward Conrud, "Unintended Consequences"

CHAPTER 28: FREDDIE SCANDAL

1. Charles Duhigg, "Pressure to Take More Risks," Syron fired David Androkonis, New York Ties, October, 5, 2008

CHAPTER 29: FANNIE EXPLODES IN SCANDAL

1. Quote by Franklin Raines about risk, Business Week, June, 2003
2. Senator Kit Bond's letter found on Fannie Mae computer, Gretchen Morgenson, Josh Rosner, "Reckless Endangerment"

CHAPTER 31: THE REPEAL OF THE GLASS-STEAGALL ACT

CHAPTER 32: COMMODITIES FUTURES TRADING COMMISSION

CHAPTER 33: MARK TO MARKET

CHAPTER 34: THE PANIC BEGINS

CHAPTER 35: FANNIE AND FREDDIE SIGNS OF TROUBLE

CHAPTER 36: THE SEC SUES FANNIE AND FREDDIE

analysts, risk managers, rating agencies and even financial regulators of vital data about market risks that could have prevented this crisis."

CHAPTER 37: FINANCIAL CRISIS INQUIRY COMMISSION

1. Paul Sperry references Angelides and Greenlining Institute
2. Peter Wallison, "one of the many myths about the Financial Crisis is that Wall Street banks led the way." "The Dissent from the Majority Report of The Financial Crisis Inquiry Commission" Peter J. Wallison

CHAPTER 39. THE NATIONALIZATION OF AMERICAN BANKS

1. John Allison, BB&T, the threat if refused TARP
2. Thomas Sowell references bank failures in depression, "The Housing Boom and Bust"
3. Senator Schumer's letter regarding Indy Mac Bank. Sheila Bair, FDIC chairman, "Bull by the Horns"
4. John Allison references Washington Mutual's bond holders

CHAPTER 40: THE DEATH STAR

1. Sheila Bair "if Citi had not been in trouble" Bair, Bull by the Horns"
2. Bair, "Citibank NA a dumping ground for toxic assets," Bair, Bull by the Horns"
3. Bair references Structured Investment Vehicles, SIVs
4. Paulson wrote Sheila Bair suggested Citi go through receivership. Henry Paulson "On the Brink"
5. Sheila Bair, "Bull by the Horns

CHAPTER 41: DODD-FRANK

1. John McCain "Bought and Paid For" Charles Gasparino
2. Joe Biden
3. Obama speech, Costa Mesa, California, March, 2009
4. Irving Fisher quote, "stock market prices have reached what looks like a permanently high plateau." The Making of Modern Economics" Mark Skousen
5. John Maynard Keynes quote, "we will not have any more crashes in out time" The Making of Modern Economics" Mark Skousen

6. Nancy Teeters, Governor Federal Reserve, quote referencing Penn Square "Secrets of the Temple" William Grieder
7. David Nason "the full guaranty" Henry Paulson "On the Brink
8. Henry Paulson

CHAPTER 42: ABOLISH THE OCC AND THE FDIC

1. Martin Mayer "The Bankers"

EPILOGUE

1. Paul Sperry "The Great American Bank Robbery

Appendix I

Federal Banking Laws

1791 Bank of United States

1816 Second Bank of the United States

1863 National Bank Act

1908 Aldrich-Vreeland Act/National Monetary Commission

1913 Federal Reserve Act

1927 McFadden Act

1933 Glass-Steagall Act

1933 Home Ownders Loan Corp

1938 Fannie Mae, amendment to the National Housing Act, 1834

1968 Fair Housing, amendment VIII to the Civil Rights Act of 1964

1970 Emergency Housing Financial Act, creation Freddie Mac and privatization

1972 Community Re-investment Act, CRA

1975 Home Mortgage Disclosure Act HMDA

1977 NOW Accounts

1977 Housing and Community Development Act, prohibits discrimination

1978 Humphrey-Hawkins Act, Federal Reserve Chair report to Congress

1980 Depository Institutions Monetary Control Act DIDMcA, deregulation S&Ls

1982   Garn-St Germain deregulation S&Ls

1989   Financial Institutions Reform, Recovery, Discovery, and Enforcement Act FIRREA deregulation S&Ls

1991   FDIC Improvement Act FDICIA in response to S&L crisis FDIC required to use least cost resolution short of liquidation the exception if a financial institution posed a "systemic" risk to economy Paulson used the exception for the first time in our history regarding the possible failure of Wachovia, page 316 "On the Brink"

1992   GSE Act or the Federal Enterprises Financial Safety and Soundness Act HUD Secretary given authority to set affordable housing goals

1994   Riegle-Neal Interstate Banking and Efficiency Act

1999   GBL or the Financial Services Modernization Act repeal of Glass-Steagall

2008   Emergency Stabilization Act $700 billion Treasury fund

2008   Troubled Asset Relief Program TARP, authority to seize any financial institutions at any price

2012   Dodd-Frank/Wall Street Reform and Consumer Protection Act

Appendix II

Dodd-Frank

The Financial Stability Oversight Council (FSOC)

Members:

Secretary of the Treasury, Chair
Chair Federal Reserve Board
Comptroller of the Currency
Chair, FDIC
Chair, SEC
Director, FHA
Chair, National Credit Union Administrator
Director, Bureau of Consumer Finance Protection
Chair, Commodities Futures Trading Commission
An independent member with insurance expertise

Appendix III

The Financial Crisis Inquiry Commission

The Financial Crisis Inquiry Commission had ten members; six were appointed by Senate Majority Leader Harry Reid and Speaker Nancy Pelosi:

Phil Angelides, Chairman (Reid and Pelosi)
Brooksley Born (Pelosi)
Robert Gramm (Reid)
Heather Murren (Reid)
John Thomson (Pelosi)

Four were appointed by Minority Leader Mitch McConnell and John Boehner:

William Thomas, Vice Chairman (McConnell and Boehner)
Keith Hennesey (McConnell)
Douglas Holtz-Eakin (McConnell)
Peter Wallison (Boehner)

Index

K

L

M

N

Forrest Russell Cook, Senior Vice President at State Street Bank
Photo by Bachrach

Original banking floor at 53 State Street

Current State Street headquarters

Granite Trust, the predecessor of South Shore Bank

Bank of New Hampshire, Manchester, New Hampshire, 1978

About the Author

Forrest Cook was a senior vice president and retail division head at State Street Bank in Boston. He served on the senior management committee and long range planning committee. He was one of the senior officers who was instrumental in the transition of an old-line Boston bank to a more entrepreneurial organization.

Cook recommended State Street's entry into bank credit cards, which greatly expanded the bank's retail base and competitive position. It also was the beginning of the evolution of electronic banking.

He later served as president and chief executive officer of South Shore Bank in Quincy, Massachusetts. South Shore was a highly regarded regional bank that covered a large territory from Boston to Rhode Island and Cape Cod. South Shore also owned a mortgage company.

Cook experienced many changes in the banking world during his career, including the government dismantling of the residential mortgage market. He decided the story of banking and the housing collapse that led to the Financial Crisis needed to be told by someone who actually ran a large bank and mortgage company.

Cook graduated from Bowdoin College, was the class president in Rutgers University Stonier Graduate School of Banking, and was the class treasurer in Harvard Business School Advanced Management. He was a second lieutenant in the army and served six years in the reserve as captain. He resides in New England with his family.

CPSIA information can be obtained at www.ICGtesting.com
Printed in the USA
BVOW08s0337130216

436599BV00002B/109/P